The
Mystery
of Death

*Goodbye, Planet Earth, It's
been nice knowing you!*

The Mystery of Death

*Goodbye, Planet Earth, It's
been nice knowing you!*

Lester Sumrall

New Leaf Press

First printing: October 1995

ISBN: 0-89221-300-0
Library of Congress Catalog: 95-69896

All Scripture quotations are from the King James
Version of the Bible unless otherwise noted.

Contents

Contents

Introduction

I have seen many tombs.
In my travels to 119 nations, I have visited:

- the tombs of the emperors in Beijing, China
- the tomb of Lenin, the father of modern Communism in Moscow
- the tomb of Napoleon in Paris
- the tombs of the kings and queens of England
- the tomb of King David
- the tomb of Abraham in the cave of Machpelah
- the tombs of the pharaohs of

Egypt — the Pyramids
- the tomb of George Washington in Virginia
- the tomb of Abraham Lincoln in Illinois

Of one thing we can be sure: Man is born to die.

No brilliance of mind and invention, no goodness of individuals, and no power or strength can keep man alive on earth indefinitely.

In his book, *How We Die*, Sherwin B. Nuland says, "We have changed the face of death."[1]

I disagree. The face of death has not changed. The power of life and death is in God's hands and will remain there until the final enemy — death — is defeated by Christ.

Death, so repulsive and terrible, was brought into the world through man's rebellion, aided by the lies of Satan. Until we understand that there are consequences for our behavior, we will never understand death.

Death Statistics

How many humans can expect to die? Every single one. All humans die.

Basically, the death rate is at 100 percent. No amount of money or research or wishing it so will keep death from claiming us.

Death is universal. Death is also democratic, having no respect for race, class, religion, or position. Every second, every minute, every hour, every day, people are leaving this world for the next.

Almost two million human beings die every week on planet Earth, but such statistics do not move us unless it affects us personally. Death does not deeply concern the human family until it draws near enough to take a loved one or a close friend. Then suddenly, the reality of death becomes apparent.

When the presence of death has drawn near, the mind begins to perceive its reality, saying, "I shall never see this loved one again on this earth," or, "I will never be able to talk again with this friend."

Many times I've seen spouses cling to their deceased beloved's casket and cry hysterically over their permanent loss. When death strikes home, those left behind must face the reality of the curse brought upon every living person in the human race.

For those who have no hope of heaven, eternal separation is an inevitable fact. It is this finality of death that throws a wet blanket of fear and dread over mankind's brief stay on earth.

Death — A Popular Subject

In recent years, death has become one of

the most popular subjects in universities and a favorite topic of book publishers.

Why this sudden interest in death? Probably because the "baby boomer" generation is beginning to feel its mortality.

One young man recently told me that when his grandfather died, he realized his generation's turn was coming up. It was the first time he had thought about the fact that he would not live forever.

There are books on how to die and how to deal with the death of loved ones; books on what happens after death and books on common deaths and uncommon deaths. There are even books on what people say and do before they die.

Almost all of these books give a clinical, and in some cases, entertaining account of the mystery of death. The authors, however, find it impossible to put a positive spin on death, leaving the reader without any offer of hope.

Few secular books research the greatest source of information available on the subject of death — the Bible. Death is mentioned hundreds of times in the King James Version of the Bible.

The Grim Reaper

In my 65 years of ministry, I've seen death up close on many occasions. I've been with folks who died alone and with those who died surrounded by loved ones. I've seen people die peacefully as they were taken into the arms of the Saviour, and I've watched dying souls writhe in agony when the monster death comes to take them.

Death is often called "the Grim Reaper," and people will do almost anything to escape it.

The elaborate burial rituals of the ancient Egyptians provide a reminder of how man will do almost anything to convince himself that death is not final.

Today people have concocted new ways of trying to cheat death. Some hope to escape planet Earth and migrate to other planets to live forever. Humanistic thought presents the lie that man can create his own reality — if you don't like what's on the other side, you can change it.

Cryogenics — the freezing of human beings — has actually been tried by patients and doctors who believe that life can be put on hold. The patient hopes to be thawed out at some point in the future and awake when medical science has the ability to cure heart disease, cancer, or whatever.

A few years ago, a 5,000-year-old man was found in the Swiss Alps. He had been frozen in ice, possibly instantly. Dead for 50 centuries, he still has not moved a muscle on his own.

People of wealth have always tried to cheat death. But all their money does not amount to a hill of beans when death comes to get them.

Only two men were "taken" without physical death — Enoch and Elijah. We know little about Enoch, but the Bible clearly states that God took him to heaven without physical death (Heb. 11:5). Elijah's exit was more dramatic as he ascended to heaven in a flaming whirlwind (2 Kings 2:1). We are not told if there were witnesses to Enoch's exit, but Elijah's successor, Elisha, did see his mentor ascend to heaven. If you believe the Bible, these accounts are not doubtful.

We can't escape death. But we can come to a place of not fearing it — if we put our trust in Jesus Christ.

[1]Sherwin B. Nuland, *How We Die* (New York, NY: First Vintage Books, 1995).

Chapter
1

How Death Had Its Beginning

Everything existing on this earth had a beginning.

Man had a beginning.

The animals had a beginning.

The flowers had a beginning.

The mountains had a beginning.

Death had a beginning.

When God was finished with his magnificent creation, He pronounced it all "very good." Death had not yet marred God's perfect masterpiece.

> And the Lord God planted a
> garden eastward in Eden; and there
> he put the man whom he had
> formed.
>
> And out of the ground made
> the Lord God to grow every tree
> that is pleasant to the sight, and
> good for food; the tree of life also
> in the midst of the garden, and the
> tree of knowledge of good and evil
> (Gen. 2:8-9).
>
> And the Lord God took the
> man, and put him into the garden
> of Eden to dress it and to keep it
> (Gen. 2:15).

In the midst of the beautiful Garden of Eden,
Adam had the privilege of rare earthly fellowship with his Creator. The Bible tells us that they
walked together in the cool of the evening. During these times, God communicated to His created being in a most unique way.

But God gave Adam a strict warning — that
death would result if he chose to go against His
wishes.

> And the Lord God commanded
> the man, saying, Of every tree of
> the garden thou mayest freely eat:

> But of the tree of the knowl-
> edge of good and evil, thou shalt
> not eat of it: for in the day that thou
> eatest thereof thou shalt surely die
> (Gen. 2:16-17).

God spent endless hours teaching Adam about His ways. More than any other man, except Jesus, Adam knew God most intimately. He was not ignorant of God's character or His commands. If there were any doubts, Adam had every opportunity to fully understand the consequences of disobedience — "thou shalt surely die."

Even before Eve was created, God had given Adam this warning about the dangers of committing the ultimate transgression. As Eve's husband, Adam was obligated to *teach* her about the one forbidden thing, not just *tell* her.

Adam was the midwife, the ultimate means, through whom Death was delivered on this planet. Adam, not Eve, was responsible for death becoming the curse of mankind. He had received his orders firsthand from the Creator and fully understood the consequences of disobedience.

A Legacy of Death

The Bible tells us that Adam was *with* Eve when she was tempted by the serpent. She didn't have to search high and low for her husband or argue and cajole him into compliance. He went along without much persuasion, leaving Adam without excuse and sharing the blame.

> And when the woman saw that
> the tree was good for food, and that
> it was pleasant to the eyes, and a
> tree to be desired to make one wise,
> she took of the fruit thereof, and did
> eat, and gave also unto her husband
> with her; and he did eat (Gen. 3:6).

When Eve ate the forbidden fruit, Adam chose her over God. He cast his lot with Eve instead of refusing to become involved in what he knew was total disobedience. Eve became Adam's god at that point, and anything put ahead of God becomes an idol.

Adam was the first to change "the truth of God into a lie" and worship and serve "the creature more than the Creator" (Rom. 1:25).

What is the fate of idolaters? They "shall have their part in the lake which burneth with fire and brimstone: which is the second death" (Rev. 21:8).

When Adam and Eve ate of the forbidden tree, their sin — which was idolatry at its worst — brought the curse of death upon their descendants.

Thou shalt have no other gods before me.

Thou shalt not make unto thee any graven image, or any likeness of any thing that is in heaven above, or that is in the earth beneath, or that is in the water under the earth:

Thou shalt not bow down thyself to them, nor serve them: for I the Lord thy God am a jealous God, visiting the iniquity of the fathers upon the children unto the third and fourth generation of them that hate me (Exod. 20:3-5).

This horrible legacy of death was passed on to Adam and Eve's children, beginning with their two oldest sons — Cain and Abel.

Death's First Victim

Death's first victim was not the parents who rebelled and disobeyed God, nor the oldest son who became the first murderer. Death's first victim was the good son, the innocent one who was obedient to God and, apparently, to his parents.

The argument between the brothers was not politics or money or family inheritances. The controversy was over religion. The self-righteous one killed the one who followed the

Spirit of God. Cain, the elder, struck and killed Abel, the younger, out of religious envy and jealousy.

> In the course of time Cain brought some of the fruits of the soil as an offering to the Lord. But Abel brought fat portions from some of the firstborn of his flock. The Lord looked with favor on Abel and his offering, but on Cain and his offering he did not look with favor. So Cain was very angry, and his face was downcast.
>
> Then the Lord said to Cain, "Why are you angry? Why is your face downcast? If you do what is right, will you not be accepted? But if you do not do what is right, sin is crouching at your door; it desires to have you, but you must master it."
>
> Now Cain said to his brother Abel, "Let's go out to the field." And while they were in the field, Cain attacked his brother Abel and killed him (Gen. 4:3-8;NIV).

That pattern has been repeated ever since. The most glaring example is that of the Pharisees — the "older brothers" — who were responsible for the crucifixion of Jesus by the Romans.

On the day Abel was murdered, Adam and Eve learned what God meant when He said, "You will surely die." They became acutely aware of the price their disobedience had exacted as they gazed in horror at the bloody, limp body of their precious son.

Abel was the first human to experience death.

Adam and Eve were the first to witness the decomposition of dead human flesh. No doubt the shell of Abel's corpse puzzled them for some time.

Scripture does not provide us with an account of this scene, but the death of their son surely brought the reality and finality of death home to Adam and Eve.

Since that time, death has been not only an ever-present fact of human life, but an enigma — something mankind has wondered about, attempted to figure out, and tried to find some way to circumvent.

Death does not always come to those who are sick or old and wanting to leave this earth. Death does not often come as a friend.

Men die because of evil and because of being separated from God through sin.

The Source of Rebellion

Death was brought to this planet by a spirit of rebellion against the Most High. What was the source of this spirit of rebellion? It existed in the person of Lucifer, the "covering cherub," who attempted to unseat Almighty God.

> How you have fallen from heaven, O morning star, son of the dawn! You have been cast down to the earth, you who once laid low the nations!
>
> You said in your heart, "I will ascend to heaven; I will raise my throne above the stars of God; I will sit enthroned on the mount of assembly, on the utmost heights of the sacred mountain.
>
> I will ascend above the tops of the clouds; I will make myself like the Most High."
>
> But you are brought down to the grave, to the depths of the pit (Isa. 14:12-15;NIV).

Lucifer, the most evil of all creatures, brought death to God's perfect creation. Knowing his destiny is hell, he sought to infiltrate God's ranks and sabotage God's purposes for man by turning Adam into a traitor .

> Now the serpent was more subtil than any beast of the field which the Lord God had made. And he said unto the woman, Yea, hath God said, Ye shall not eat of every tree of the garden?
> And the woman said unto the serpent, We may eat of the fruit of the trees of the garden:
> But of the fruit of the tree which is in the midst of the garden, God hath said, Ye shall not eat of it, neither shall ye touch it, lest ye die.
> And the serpent said unto the woman, Ye shall not surely die:
> For God doth know that in the day ye eat thereof, then your eyes shall be opened, and ye shall be as gods, knowing good and evil (Gen. 3:1-5).

Lucifer corrupted God's most impressive creation — man — by continuing to tell him that if he challenged God, he would *not* die! Why did Adam believe this "father of lies"? Because, like you and me, Adam and Eve were full of pride. They accepted this direct contradiction against God's wishes with less than a moment's consideration of the final consequences.

Adam and Eve's one act of rebellion against the loving God of creation brought sin into the world and death as its final punishment.

> Wherefore, as by one man sin entered into the world, and death by sin; and so death passed upon all men, for that all have sinned (Rom. 5:12).

By "one man's offence death reigned" (Rom. 5:17). Satan knew that all he had to do was get the first man to listen to him and the rest would follow.

> By the offence of one judgment came upon all men to condemnation. . . .
> For as by one man's disobedience many were made sinners. . . .
> That as sin hath reigned unto death (Rom. 5:18-19, 21).

Although death's reign on the earth began in the Garden, Adam lived 930 years before he finally died. The rebellion, which had been bred in the heart of man by the father of the human race, did not subside. Instead, man after man continued to rebel against his Creator and gravitate toward the evil one.

> The earth also was corrupt before God, and the earth was filled with violence.
> And God looked upon the earth, and, behold, it was corrupt; for all flesh had corrupted his way upon the earth (Gen. 6:11-12).

Over the next 700 years, the filthy heart of man had become so wicked and disgusting to God that He decided to wipe out the world's population at that time — except for Noah and his family.

> And God saw that the wickedness of man was great in the earth, and that every imagination of the thoughts of his heart was only evil continually.
> And it repented the Lord that he had made man on the earth, and it grieved him at his heart.
> And the Lord said, I will destroy man whom I have created from the face of the earth; both man, and beast, and the creeping thing, and the fowls of the air; for it repenteth me that I have made them.

> But Noah found grace in the
> eyes of the Lord (Gen. 6:5-8).

For over 100 years, God restrained the consuming hand of death, as Noah and his three sons built an ark.

> And God said unto Noah, The
> end of all flesh is come before me;
> for the earth is filled with violence
> through them; and, behold, I will
> destroy them with the earth (Gen.
> 6:13).

Imagine Satan's delight at the prospect of God's initially joyful relationship with man coming to an end. Satan, seeing this as another opportunity to sabotage God's plan for mankind, whispered to Noah's congregations in the shadow of the ark, "Don't believe him. Noah is a fool. You won't die. It's not going to rain. Who ever heard of a flood in the desert?"

Satan's deception was effective because on that day when the fountains of the deep were broken up and the rains fell, there was both instant and slow death all over the face of the earth. Mass confusion and horror reigned. God's patience had run out. Death reigned on the earth.

They rose greatly on the earth, and all the high mountains under the entire heavens were covered. The waters rose and covered the mountains to a depth of more than twenty feet. Every living thing that moved on the earth perished — birds, livestock, wild animals, all the creatures that swarm over the earth, and all mankind. Everything on dry land that had the breath of life in its nostrils died. Every living thing on the face of the earth was wiped out; men and animals and the creatures that move along the ground and the birds of the air were wiped from the earth. Only Noah was left, and those with him in the ark.

The waters flooded the earth for a hundred and fifty days (Gen. 7:19-24;NIV).

Man was given another chance to follow God's ways and establish a world of peace and righteousness. Even the Creator, however, realized that "the imagination of man's heart is evil from his youth" (Gen. 8:21).

It was at this point that God saw the need to limit man's life span — and his ability to pass on his wicked ways. Up until the Flood, some people had lived for centuries. The fifth chapter of Genesis lists the accounts of several men who lived more than 900 years on the earth. The longest living man was Methuselah, who lived 969 years (Gen. 5:27).

Just before the Flood, God decided, because of man's propensity for wickedness, to limit his years on earth to 120 (Gen. 6:3).

In spite of the reduced life span, the new beginning set forth by God after the Flood didn't last long. Pagan cities like Babylon sprang up and were used by Satan as training grounds for future corruption. Humanistic thought — that man is god — had its start in ancient Babylon and continues to spread its message of death today.

The Separation

When Adam and Eve were first created on this planet, God lived in His heaven but came down and walked in the Garden in the "cool of the day" to visit with and commune with Adam (Gen. 3:8).

Adam and Eve may not have been in the literal presence of God all of the time, but they were not "separated" from Him. His life — called "zoe" in the Greek — was part of them until their pride, self-will, and rebellion shut God out.

Once the life of man was separated from the

life of God, something vital ended. This separating of the spiritual realm from the natural realm affected all life on earth. It even affected the planet itself.

God created man to live forever. Death was not a part of God's original creation. Man, through the influence of Satan, introduced death into a perfect planetary system. As a result, man has to bear the brunt of, and live with the consequences of, the terrible original sin of rebellion.

Why do people attempt to get away from God?

There are so many evidences that a supreme God has designed all of us and everything we see — and many things we don't. Yet, otherwise intelligent men and women constantly push thoughts of a judging God out of their minds.

All of us, at one time or another, have denied God and run from Him. Many turn around and run toward him, but many more still flee.

A day is coming when men will actually run toward death. That's how terrible conditions on planet Earth will become. By their previous denial of God, however, they won't find any relief from their torment.

> And in those days shall men
> seek death, and shall not find it; and
> shall desire to die, and death shall

flee from them (Rev. 9:6).

Life and Death

Immortality begins with life.

Life, however, is the greatest mystery in our world. There are many mysteries surrounding mankind, but the greatest is how two protoplasmic cells unite and generate life.

God, who is the giver of all life, permitted man to join Him in divinity and in the mystery of life.

The Lord Jesus Christ said, "I am the way, the truth, and the life" (John 14:6). Jesus is life because He is God!

In God's eyes life is sacred because it is immortal. That is why the act of reproduction of human life and the sacredness of "reproducing after its kind" is so closely guarded by God.

God makes clear the consequences that come to those who have no respect for the act of reproduction:

> But whoso committeth adultery with a woman lacketh understanding: he that doeth it destroyeth his own soul.
>
> A wound and dishonour shall he get; and his reproach shall not be wiped away (Prov. 6:32-33).

God warns that if you trifle with the elements of immortality, it is like putting your fingers on a hot stove — you get burned.

During World War II, the beasts who ran the Third Reich enjoyed what they thought was the power of life and death over whole countries. In reality, they did not control anything. They had allowed themselves to believe they held the keys to immortality for all people, particularly the Jews. Hitler, Himmler, and Goering all loved inflicting death. They could merely speak a word, and thousands would die.

Throughout history, men have lusted after a fascination with inflicting death. That longing is satanic.

Death is used by Satan, but its control is in the hands of God.

God Almighty, however, is the giver of life. His mind is infinite, and our minds are finite. That's why we grope for answers to monsters like Hitler, Himmler, and Goering who themselves could not escape death. All three committed suicide.

But where are the high-ranking Nazis today? Those who have died physical deaths because of rebellion against God will end up going where "death" goes. This is called the second death.

He that hath an ear, let him hear

what the Spirit saith unto the churches; He that overcometh shall not be hurt of the second death. . . .

And death and hell were cast into the lake of fire. This is the second death.

And whosover was not found written in the book of life was cast into the lake of fire (Rev. 2:11; 20:14-15).

Death had a beginning, and death will have an end. Death was born in the Garden of Eden, and death will die in the lake of fire.

The Iron Curtain of Death

In 1946, Sir Winston Churchill gave a speech at Fulton, Missouri, in which he described the Soviet grip on Europe as "an iron curtain." At that time, Joseph Stalin's reign of terror in eastern Europe was just beginning and became a curtain of death that separated East from West.

In the 1980s, Communism's death grip was loosened, and the Iron Curtain came down as the Berlin Wall crumbled piece by piece before our eyes.

Death, however, closes the curtain on life permanently. There will be no reprieve for lost souls after the final death. There will be no tearing down of the great wall that will separate life from death.

Death is an attempt to destroy the creation brought forth by Almighty God. Satan, who is alive today, introduced death.

The Bible says that the last enemy to be destroyed is death. That is when man will be restored to his original state and fellowship with God for eternity.

When God breathed into Adam, the creature was designed to live forever in fellowship with God. Earth was in harmony with heaven. God walked with man.

The Bible tells us of a time when God will restore man to his original state to live in fellowship with Him forever (2 Cor. 5:17-21). For those who have accepted Jesus Christ as personal Saviour, there will be no second death, or eternity away from God. The curtain of death will be rent in two.

Death Defined

Death is a cold word, a word with no sweetness. Death says, "Someone does not live here anymore."

Death is no respecter of persons — or schedules.

I was in Tokyo when my mother died at the age of 87.

I was in Singapore when Leona, my sister, died. Leona had traveled with me when I was a teenage evangelist in the South.

My father, my half sister Anna, and my sister Louise already had preceded Mother to the other side, as had my older half brothers, Houston and Kerney.

In the fall of 1993, the only remaining member of my immediate family — my oldest brother, Ernest — made the transition to the next world. There were three girls and four boys born in my family. Now I alone am left.

It was very hard to preach that week, the first Sunday of my life that I had no family living on planet Earth. I have my own family, but my father's family is all gone.

In May 1994 my beloved wife of almost 50 years, Louise, who had been by my side in ministry for all of those years, went to be with the Lord.

I can understand the one who said, "And I am the only one who has escaped to tell you!" (Job 1:15;NIV).

As a young man, if you would have told me that one day I would be left alone on this earth with not one of my immediate family living and my wife gone on ahead of me, I would not have believed it nor accepted it. There was nothing to indicate that I would be the one to outlive everyone in my family.

With the passing of these dear loved ones, however, I have come to understand and accept death in a new light. Death is not an ending of life, but merely a transition to a new and different life.

Falling Asleep in Jesus

Those of us left behind by loved ones and

friends who have moved on ahead of us are happy for them to be at peace. We are happy for them to be in a place without trouble, sorrow, and hardships. Most of all, we ourselves also yearn to be in the presence of Jesus. At the same time, our souls are lonely and miss the everyday comfort of being able to reach out and touch or talk with those who have passed on.

In the Word of God, however, there is comfort. The gentle, kind Holy Spirit moved many writers to talk of death in ways that make clear it is only a door to another world, a transition to a better life for those who belong to the family of God. That is why the Bible speaks of death as "falling asleep."

> And the Lord said unto Moses,
> Behold, thou shalt sleep with thy
> fathers (Deut. 31:16).

The apostle Paul wrote the same of early Christians who saw Jesus after His resurrection:

> After that, he was seen of
> above five hundred brethren at
> once; of whom the greater part re-
> main unto this present, but some are
> fallen asleep (1 Cor. 15:6).

Other synonyms for death are "giving up

the ghost" and being "gathered to one's people."

> Then Abraham gave up the ghost, and died in a good old age, an old man, and full of years; and was gathered to his people (Gen. 25:8).

> And Isaac gave up the ghost, and died, and was gathered unto his people, being old and full of days: and his sons Esau and Jacob buried him (Gen. 35:29).

Many years after Jacob and Esau stood by their father's grave in the Cave of Machpelah, Jacob "yielded" up the ghost, "gathered up his feet into the bed" and was "gathered unto his people" (Gen. 49:33).

Perhaps the closest synonym is that death is a change.

> If a man die, shall he live again? all the days of my appointed time will I wait, till my change come (Job 14:14).

The apostle Peter, knowing his time on earth was about over, said that he must shortly "put off this my tabernacle" (2 Pet. 1:14). Peter said he was following the example shown him by the Lord Jesus Christ.

The Psalmist called death going down into silence (Ps. 115:17) Job referred to this transition as going the way from which he would not return (Job 16:22) and fleeing as a shadow and continuing not (Job 14:2).

A Matter of Life and Death

Today the dying are usually unconscious or heavily medicated when death takes them. Years ago, however, it was common for family and friends to glimpse a departing loved one's vision of the afterlife. In days gone by, vivid descriptions of heaven and hell were told.

I have seen men scream as death claimed them.

I have also seen many folks pass blissfully away into eternity.

I was told of a lady who, as she lay dying, asked a friend of mine, "Do you think there is music in heaven?"

He answered, "Yes, I think there is."

"Well," she said with a smile, "I can hear it." She also told my friend that she could see her husband who had gone on before.

I have no experience in that realm. I have asked for such visions but have not yet received any.

Peaceful and free — that's the way to die

— peaceful in Jesus.

There is a difference between the death of the righteous and those who receive death as the wages of sin — a sentence pronounced over all who have descended from Adam.

The prophet Balaam desired to receive the "death of the righteous" as Jacob had:

> Who can count the dust of Jacob, and the number of the fourth part of Israel? Let me die the death of the righteous, and let my last end be like his (Num. 23:10).

What was Jacob's death like? Apparently, he died as the Psalmist wrote in Psalm 37:37:

> Mark the perfect man, and behold the upright: for the end of that man is peace.

The apostle Paul wrote that "the wages of sin is death" but eternal life through Jesus is a gift of God (Rom. 6:23).

What is sin? Sin is following a way that seems right to men, but if that way is against God, it becomes the "way of death." In the end, that way brings a payoff in not just physical death but eternal separation from God.

There is a way which seemeth
right unto a man, but the end
thereof are the ways of death
(Prov. 14:12).

God, however, is not happy about those who
choose the way of death. He is not vindictive,
but He is just.

Say unto them, As I live, saith
the Lord God, I have no pleasure
in the death of the wicked; but that
the wicked turn from his way [the
path that leads to receiving the
wages of sin] and live: turn ye, turn
ye from your evil ways; for why
will ye die, O house of Israel?
(Ezek. 33:11).

Man's choice of sin over righteousness takes
him down the pathway to death.

It has been said that Lenin, on his deathbed,
screamed for days before the Monster claimed
him.

Death stalked Hitler for years before the
Nazi dictator shot himself in 1945. Former sec-
retaries describe frantic nightmares that hounded
this ruthless man of evil.

Death is closer than some of us realize.

The Way of Peace

For a born-again person, there is no fear of death. If fear is present in such a person, it is because they are not living in all of the inheritance provided them by Jesus on the cross.

One reason that Jesus visited earth was to bring peace of mind about living and dying.

> Through the tender mercy of our God; whereby the dayspring from on high hath visited us,
> To give light to them that sit in darkness and in the shadow of death, to guide our feet into the way of peace (Luke 1:78-79).

The "way of peace" is not to live in the shadow caused by the fear of death. Once a person belongs to Jesus, there is no more "sting of death," which is caused by fear.

Some have said that a person who has died to sin by receiving Jesus (Rom. 8:2) has died all the death he is ever going to undergo. Why is that? Because a born-again person does not experience the ending of life when he leaves earth. He experiences the real beginning of life.

Shortly before his physical death, the apostle Paul knew when the time came for him to make this transition. He said he was ready to go and looking forward to it.

For I am now ready to be of-
fered, and the time of my departure
is at hand.

I have fought a good fight, I
have finished my course, I have
kept the faith:

Henceforth there is laid up for
me a crown of righteousness, which
the Lord, the righteous judge, shall
give me at that day: and not to me
only, but unto all them also that love
his appearing (2 Tim. 4:6-8).

Other Kinds of Death

Death does not always mean the death of
the body. Other things die: visions, dreams,
hopes, churches, ministries, marriages, and even
societies.

In the United States, many historians and
analysts of society believe America is "dying."
William J. Bennett, United States Secretary of
Education for three years under President
Reagan, says we are not in danger of being defeated by Communism, or from outside, but from
within.

The late scholar and author Walker Percy
said that death of our society is being revealed
by the symptoms of boredom, cynicism, greed,
few restraints on self-interest, and less value

placed on moral obligations, much less moral values.[1]

Another symptom of death in society is the merchandising of everything. Love and death have been turned into the "coin of the realm" and, thereby, have lost much of their significance.

A kind of death is found in the spoken word, the fruit of the tongue — according to King Solomon whose wisdom was collected in the Book of Proverbs.

> Death and life are in the power of the tongue: and they that love it shall eat the fruit thereof (Prov. 18:21).

James expanded on this truth in the New Testament.

> Even so the tongue is a little member, and boasteth great things. Behold, how great a matter a little fire kindleth!
>
> And the tongue is a fire, a world of iniquity: so is the tongue among our members, that it defileth the whole body, and setteth on fire the course of nature; and it is set on fire of hell. . . .
>
> Out of the same mouth pro-

ceedeth blessing and cursing. My brethren, these things ought not so to be (James 3:5-6, 10).

You can "kill" attitudes, projects, abilities, and hope through words spoken unwisely, sharply, or with malice. James calls this kind of speech "full of deadly poison" (James 3:8).

Death Defined

Dictionary definitions of death include: decease, demise, mortality, extinction, dissolution, departure, release, eternal rest, cessation (loss or extinction) of life, and the tomb or the grave.

In the Bible, there are a number of words in Hebrew and Greek that denote death in its various forms. In the *Hebrew and Chaldee Dictionary* of *Strong's Concordance,*[2] we find:

- *Muwth,* a primitive root, meaning "to die," or "to kill, to be dead, to slay, to destroy" (4191, p. 63).
- *Muwth-labben,* "to die for" (4192, p. 64).
- *Maveth,* natural or violent death, the place or state of the dead, and used figuratively, pestilence or ruin (4194, p. 64).
- *Ratsach,* another primitive root

word meaning "to dash in pieces," in other words, "to kill" (especially used for murder), "to put to death," or for manslayer or murderer (7523, p. 110).

In Strong's *Greek Dictionary of the New Testament,* the words for death are:

- *Anaireo,* meaning "to take up," or by implication, "to take away violently" (337, p. 11).
- *Apokteino,* two other words meaning "to slay" make this word, defined as "to kill outright," or figuratively "to destroy, to put to death, to kill, to slay" (615, p. 14).
- *Eschatos,* an adverb meaning "finally," or "at the extremity of life — point of death" (2079, p. 33).
- *Thanatos,* an adjective used as a noun, meaning "death," literally or figuratively (2288 and 2289, p. 35).
- *Teleute,* meaning decease, from teleutao, meaning "to finish life, to expire, to be dead" (5054, 5053, p. 71).

All of these definitions are used in both literal and figurative senses. For example, there is a kind or type of sorrow that brings death.

The apostle Paul wrote to the Corinthian Christians about two kinds of sorrow. There is the kind that works good and the kind that works death.

> For godly sorrow worketh repentance to salvation not to be repented of: but the sorrow of the world worketh death (2 Cor. 7:10).

Death can be summed up as the ending of something. When anything dies, some kind of "life" is over.

A Snap of the Fingers

In spite of having lived into my eighth decade, my time on earth seems "fleeting" to me. We are here today and gone tomorrow (Job 14:2). This life is the shadow; eternity is the reality that casts the shadow.

Life is short. It seems just yesterday I was healed of tuberculosis as a 17 year old who had chosen to preach rather than die. Today, more than 65 years later, I am still preaching the gospel.

It is hard to believe that many years have passed since I was in Tibet and mainland China when Chiang Kai-shek was fighting Imperial Japan in the east and the Communists under Mao Tse-tung in the north.

I may be left here alone on earth, but I know that my entire family has simply moved on to the place where death will never again mark even a temporary separation. My parents, my brothers and sisters, and my wife all are waiting for me in a place without time limits.

The Bible gives us a glimpse of the life to come but not a lot of specific details. Yet the span of life on earth is a snap of the fingers compared to the total duration of life. It is a "brief, fleeting instant" in contrast to the reality that has no time and no death.

Explaining Death Away

Death is the door through which corporeality enters immortality and eternity.

Various religions explain death in various ways:

1. The Hindus and other Eastern religions say human life simply is transformed into other bodies or forms. Known as transmigration and reincarnation, this is what they dreamed up to deal with knowing that life does not cease at death.

2. Animists worship inanimate objects (those without life) such as rocks, waterfalls, and trees, giving them as much importance as human life.

3. Humanism says physical death is the end.

4. Nihilism says the highest aim of life is to reach the "eternal nothingness."

5. Of the Christian sects, those following Seventh Day Adventism believe that life ends temporarily at physical death, but that in the resurrection people will not only find themselves in new physical bodies but will regain spiritual consciousness.

The Bible, God's Holy Word, teaches that death is a curtain that separates earth from heaven. As a veil through which passage is only one way, death is governed by certain "laws" that belong to God:

> He that is our God is the God of salvation; and unto God the Lord belong the issues from death (Ps. 68:20).

Where Do the Dead Go?

People of different religions have varying answers to the question, "Where do the dead go when they die?"

- The Seventh Day Adventists say the dead sleep in the earth.
- The Hindus say humans are reincarnated into another form of life.

> • Humanists say man becomes non-existent.

The apostle Paul, by divine revelation from God, tells us that the bodies of the dead who have accepted Christ will be resurrected when Jesus returns for His church. Their bodies decay in the ground right now, but their souls reside in paradise, a kind of wonderful "holding place" until after the judgment.

According to the Scriptures, the souls of those who have died rejecting Christ are sent to a place of torment.

> The wicked shall be turned into hell (Ps. 9:17).

> Whosoever was not found written in the book of life was cast into the lake of fire (Rev. 20:15).

Spiritual death is far worse than physical death. The latter lasts usually but a moment; spiritual death goes on throughout eternity. It is permanent separation from God.

The Shadow of Death

As far as death of the physical body is concerned, many people would like to believe that they can choose their destination for the eternal phase of existence. Also, they prefer to choose the quality of their transition from life to death by determining the way they deal with or pass through this final door to change.

The shadow of death that people fear, however, has a basis in reality. The Bible gives us some clear descriptions of what death is:

> Before I go whence I shall not return, even to the land of darkness and the shadow of death" (Job 10:21).

The ancient Egyptians had a consuming preoccupation with death. To them, death was a murky, dark, almost forbidding place.

We like to think of ourselves as more sophisticated today, but we're still "shadowed" by this same revulsion at the mere thought of death. In America, we try to pretend that death happens "somewhere else." At some point, however, the physical world becomes the spiritual world.

> Seek him that maketh the seven stars and Orion, and turneth the shadow of death into the morning, and maketh the day dark with night: that calleth for the waters of the sea, and poureth them out upon the face of the earth: The

Lord is his name (Amos 5:8).

The psalmist David, however, did not fear walking through the shadow of death:

> Yea, though I walk through the valley of the shadow of death, I will fear no evil: for thou art with me; thy rod and thy staff they comfort me (Ps. 23:4).

Why was David, who often faced death from his enemies, not afraid of death? Because he knew that God, who is the "Good Shepherd," would be with him even in life's last moments on earth.

In Those Final Moments

As the final moments of a person's life on this earth ebb away, regret is a familiar companion. Some of the time is spent in confession — a secret here, a secret there.

A man whose wife served God came to the door of death. Instead of accompanying her to church, this man went fishing every Sunday.

I went to his home a number of times and asked him to come to church.

"Oh no, I'm a fisherman. I don't go to church," he would say.

Then he got sick and was hospitalized. The

doctors were very honest, telling him, "You're going to die."

When I went to visit him, he said, "Preacher I need you badly. It's different this time. The doctors say I can't live."

I took his hand and put it in mine. As we prayed together, tears ran down his face. Then, he opened his eyes and said, "To think, I was going to go to hell over a six-inch fish."

I never got away from the fact that he escaped hell by coming to Jesus and remarking that a six-inch fish almost took him to eternal torment.

He never left the hospital and died a couple of days later.

Your last minute is very important, but you don't have to wait until you are on your deathbed. You can confess your sins to God today and ask His forgiveness through the shed blood of Jesus Christ. Then you, too, can escape hell and receive eternal life.

[1] William J. Bennett, "Quantifying America's Decline," *Wall Street Journal*, March 15, 1993.

[2] William Gesenius, *Hebrew and Chaldee Lexicon of the Old Testament: Numerically Coded to Strong's Exhaustive Concordance* (Grand Rapids, MI: Baker Book House/ Revell, 1984).

Chapter
3

Life after Death

In the past 20 years, a tremendous interest in life after death has surfaced — perhaps because the Church has stopped teaching about heaven. People want to know what lies behind the curtain. Hundreds of books have been written about life after death.

No one knows what death is like until he experiences it; it is a journey we all must take alone.

You may have many questions about death:

Where will I spend eternity?
Are the dead conscious right now?
Will the dead recognize one another in eternity?

Is there a choice and a chance
for salvation after death?

The greatest problems and questions regarding life after death are answered *only by the Bible*.

The destiny of man, however, cannot be changed after he breathes his last. No human being who has ever lived can change his eternal destination after death.

The Word of God says a person cannot die twice: "Man is destined to die once" (Heb. 9:27). Man cannot die twice. He does not go to hell to return to earth after a period of suffering.

There is no hope in hell.

If you live by faith in Jesus Christ, you won't have a fascination with death. You will understand death is a transition in life.

Life Never Ends

Once life begins at the conception of a child, it never ends. Everyone lives forever, the only variable is where each person will live. The only question that remains is the quality of life after death.

Aborted babies live on with Jesus.

Children who die live on with Jesus.

Young adults live on in the place where their choices for or against Jesus put them.

Old people live on in heaven or in hell.

Just as the quality of death is established by

daily choices throughout life on earth, the quality of one's life on the other side of death also is determined by one choice: accept Jesus or refuse Jesus.

The Bible says "God planted the sense of eternity into the hearts of men" (Eccles. 3:11).

Dr. Maurice Rawlings has written that this "hope of immortality" acts as a "homing" instinct.[1]

Many birds, ducks, and geese have a built-in "device" that leads them to go north or south at set times of the year. Observers can never know exactly what day that will be — but the winged birds and fowls know unerringly.

Swallows return to Capistrano, an island off the coast of California, each year on the same day. Fish will swim upstream, against the current, to return to their birthplace in order to spawn their young.

Does it seem so unlikely that the Creator built a homing device into His human creation?

The Bible tells us there *is* a place prepared for those who have accepted Jesus as the path back to God. Mankind lost its way in the Garden of Eden and, ever since, has hunted for the way back to its natural home.

That home is called "heaven," or the place where God lives. Jesus told His disciples He was going to go and "prepare" that place for them and for all of those who follow in His footsteps down through the centuries (John 14:2-3).

Why Death is Necessary

Time limits on life spans on this earth are not really "natural." Life was created to always exist and have no endings of any kind. Physical death, however, which began as a result of Adam and Eve's disobedience, can be merciful.

Without death — pain, sickness, and disease would go on forever. Without death — wickedness, abuse, murder, and warfare would continue until mankind self-destructed. In fact, mankind's demise almost occurred in Noah's day because the span of life on this earth was centuries longer than now. Again, in his mercy, God shortened the length of man's days (Gen. 6).

Without death, it would always be *now*, always present tense. That would be terrible if evil always was now.

Life is a reality; death is a temporary, practical necessity.

Death is a function of time to which all creatures now are subject. Man can hold off death, forestall death, and avoid death for certain periods of time — but time itself is one thing over which man has no control. All we can do is measure it.

God brought time into being, and God will bring time to an end (Rev. 10:5-7). Time is an artificial measure, a "lease" set to run for a preestablished number of years on this planet. When time ends, death goes with it. Life then will revert to its truly *natural* state — always present tense.

Life without death is the true reality.

Life goes on and on and on; death has a time limit.

Life begins — but life never ends.

Happy Hunting Grounds

Most ancient cultures, which were not godly at all, actually saw death closer to reality than we do today. They looked on death as simply an interruption of life, a forced change of location, and a "graduation" of sorts.

Pagan cultures were closer in time to the creation of mankind, so they retained some vestiges of truth. However, as time moved farther from Noah's day, those cultures became more and more deceived. They perverted the truth, which they did retain.

The Egyptians, one of the oldest cultures of which we have secular records, not only believed that life continued after the span of time on this earth was over, but believed it was much the same kind of life. They preserved the body, prepared things to take with them into the next great plane of existence, and even expected to eat and drink there.

The Babylonians had similar beliefs, and the

Persians thought there were good and bad locations to which one traveled. They thought that after physical death good and bad spirits fought to decide to which place you would go.

Even with all of the "philosophy and vain speculation" for which the Greeks were noted, they also believed that life goes on and on and on. They had different theories as to what happened when life ended on earth, but they had no doubt that it continued somewhere and somehow.

The beliefs of Native Americans on life after death resembled those of the Egyptians. In some tribes, warriors were buried with bows and arrows for use in the "happy hunting grounds" in the sky.

Dr. Maurice Rawlings, in *Beyond Death's Door,* writes:

> Belief in life beyond the grave is common in nearly all cultures. As one studies the history of man it is almost impossible to find a people who did not have faith in some form of existence after death.[2]

Only since Charles Darwin developed the theory of evolution and since the Age of Rationalism has there been large-scale disbelief in the life after this life. Until that time, nearly everyone in every age knew that life begins at birth and goes on forever. The only differences in opinion were how this happened, what determined where one went, and who was in charge of the future places of abode.

The Tibetans had elaborate outlines of the various stages one must go through while making the transition from life here to life there — wherever *there* was.

My Near-Death Experience

When I was 17 years old, I had tuberculosis and was in bed for several months. The medical profession, along with our family doctor, did the best they possibly could to halt my disease but found it impossible.

Day by day I was becoming weaker and weaker until finally one afternoon about four o'clock, I began to heave and spit up large amounts of blood from my lungs. I turned purple.

One of the family went quickly to get the doctor. When he arrived, he could not get a pulse reading.

The doctor turned to my parents, put his arms on their shoulders, and said, "I'm sorry to tell you that Lester will be dead in two hours' time. I must go back to the office for a while, and I will make out his death certificate. You can pick it up tomorrow morning and take it to the cemetery and purchase a lot."

My mother, a determined prayer warrior, immediately went to battle for my life.

As I lay in a rather semiconscious condition, I drifted into a vision-type experience in which I saw beside my bed an open coffin, very beautiful with fluffy satin sheets. It was balanced leaning slightly toward me as if welcoming me to come in.

The Lord spoke to me and said, "If you will preach, I will heal you."

For years, I had struggled with accepting God's call on my life. I wanted to be a hard-driving businessman like my father. I did not want to be soft and "good" like my mother — although she was the one I went to with all my problems.

I didn't want to be a preacher, so I told God, "I won't preach. In fact, I don't even like preachers."

At that point, I looked over to the other side of my bed and saw a giant Bible, reaching from the ceiling to the floor. God said, "If you will preach, I will let you live."

I refused again. Looking at the coffin on the other side of the bed, I was still unmoved. God spoke one more time: "Then, tonight, you will die."

I realized I was between a rock and a hard place. Yet, I remained stubborn.

Then a miracle took place. Inside of my

being, something came alive and I said, "God, if You would heal me, I will preach the gospel." In that moment, my life was changed, and I became a new person.

After my death-bed reprieve, I dropped off to sleep. The next morning when I awoke, my mother was hovering over me, expecting me to breath my last at any moment. After all, I was 10 or 12 hours overdue for death.

I opened my eyes and said, "I'm going to be a preacher."

Three days later, strength returned to my body. Ten days later, I went fishing in the Gulf of Mexico.

Three weeks later, God reminded me of my preaching commitment. Against my father's wishes, I packed my suitcase, left home, and never looked back.

After my near-death experience, I realized what death actually meant. It means a complete separation from family and friends. But I also began to understand the meaning of complete obedience to God.

The Land Beyond Time

Most of the Bible deals with living in the here and now. Why is that? Because the choices we make in the here and now determine where we go after death. Wondering what kind of place eternity is should not be nearly as important to us as determining where our future destination will be.

Contrary to many beliefs and speculations, there *are* only two places in which eternity is spent: heaven and hell.

Time no longer exists in either place.

Time is only an earthly boundary set to keep a wicked world system from continuing forever or from destroying all life on earth.

Someone has said that life is to be lived in three tenses: past, present, and future. We understand and deal with the past and the present. However, many people — even Christians — limit "future" to a few years of time ahead or days or weeks or hours. No one even has the promise of tomorrow still here on earth.

Future means forever, living on and on in a space where time no longer has any meaning. If folks truly understood that concept, that reality, I believe a lot of past lives would have been lived differently. A lot of the present-tense lives of people would change, and a lot of tomorrows would be lived with a desire to please the God of the universe.

Short-Term Visits

In recent years, many books and articles dealing with experiences in short-term visits into eternity have been written. It used to be that only once in a while did we hear of someone who was near death enough to see into the next realm, yet returned to tell of it. Today, many more people are experiencing this — or, at least, many more are telling of their experience.

Some have gone through the "curtain" of death and reported coming out into the glorious light and brilliance of heaven. Those who have chosen Jesus invariably do not wish to return here. The domain of God has such peace and joy that nothing on earth is more attractive.

The apostle Paul wrote of "a man he knew" (whom most Bible scholars believe was himself) who visited heaven.

> And I knew such a man, (whether in the body, or out of the body, I cannot tell: God knoweth;) How that he was caught up into paradise, and heard unspeakable words, which it is not lawful for a man to utter (2 Cor. 12:3-4).

At a later point in his life, Paul wrote that he was torn between two desires: to go on into eternity and be with Jesus, which would be better for him, or to stay and help others on earth, which would be better for them (Phil. 1:23-24).

Some have said they met Jesus in those "visits" into eternity and were filled with immeasurable ecstasy. Others testify of experiencing love as they never had on earth.

A few report actually going into hell, and their lives usually are changed when they return. Some are sent back to earth by Jesus to accomplish certain missions.

Kenneth E. Hagin, Dr. Richard E. Eby, and the late Thomas Welch, a pioneer preacher with Gordon Lindsey, are among those who have been shown the reality of hell. Welch and Hagin both saw hell, and Eby relates being shown both heaven and hell.

Some report seeing a "being of light" who tells them the Bible is inaccurate, Christians are deceived, and there is no God to judge them. These people also come back to life on earth with "missions" to spread their falsehoods.

Those who have after-death experiences and see delusions did not know Jesus before they left here and were already deceived. A person who *knows* there is a God and a devil and heaven and a hell — but has not accepted Jesus as Saviour — will not be deluded in a brief visit beyond this life.

Theirs will be a one-way ticket. They will only see hell — and not return to tell about it.

Misconceptions about Life after Death

In our culture today, we have "the science of death," in which people study all of the aspects of death of the physical body — except, of course, what the Bible says. That is like studying all about cars without ever picking up the owner's manual.

Among the misconceptions about life after death are these:

• *After physical death everyone goes to the same place.*

In other words, there is only "heaven," no "hell."

Jesus told the graphic story of the rich man and the beggar Lazarus who both died but ended up in very different places (Luke 16:20-31). This account teaches us the truth that dead people do not cease to think or feel, and the choices made during life are irrevocable.

What makes hell "hellish" is regret about things committed in life and things omitted. The biggest regret, of course, is not having accepted Jesus as Saviour.

• *Life in heaven can be earned.*

Nothing could be further from the truth! Heaven is a place you go to because it is *home*, a place that draws you because your homing device is activated.

Heaven is only home to you if you belong to Jesus. Otherwise, heaven is alien to you. In fact, the light of heaven will be unbearable to you.

• *Life in heaven is for everyone.*

This is a total deception. There are two directions in which to go once that "curtain" between this life and the next is pierced, and the choice has already been made before a person walks through the door.

• *Life in heaven is a passive, floating existence with everyone playing harps and sitting on a river bank or cloud.*

If God created man on earth to work six days and rest one, then the desire to be busy with productive labor also is part of man. Life was brought into being by God for a purpose, and throughout eternity, we will fulfill that purpose.

• *Life in the Islamic heaven is one of sensual pleasure.*

This is another deception. Flesh, or the material body, has no place in eternity. Eternal bodies are made of different material — out of substance that does not tire, does not get sick, and never gets old. Sensual or carnal attractions will not exist in the future life.

• *Life on earth can be experienced again and again, which is the belief in reincarnation.*

The Bible specifically says that it is *appointed* unto man once to die, and then comes the judgment (Heb. 9:27). Reincarnation is a counterfeit of the truth that one can be "born again" through Jesus. It attempts to make a physical explanation of a spiritual truth.

• *Life on earth is not the only time to make a choice for God.*

One religious group teaches that after a time of suffering in an interim place between heaven and hell, a person can be prayed into heaven by surviving relatives. The story Jesus told of the rich man and the poor beggar belies that. These two men were immediately in the places in eternity which their earthly choices had determined. There was no way back for the rich man and no way out of hell.

The eternal destiny of a man cannot be changed after he breathes his last breath on earth.

Without the facts in the Bible, the science of death is not a true science at all, only more vain speculations.

The Deceiving Light

As time runs out for the devil, he is stepping up his attacks on mankind on many fronts. One of the most pervasive weapons is called the New Age movement, but there is nothing "new" about it.

Nearly two millenniums ago, the apostle Paul wrote to Timothy:

Now the spirit speaketh expressly, that in the latter times some shall depart from the faith, giving heed to seducing spirits, and doctrines of devils (1 Tim. 4:1).

The Holy Ghost himself warned that in the last days some would depart from the faith.

Our faith is in the Book, the Word of God. Without the Book, we would not have any source of faith. The Bible even says that faith comes by hearing the Word of God. So, without the Word of God, we have no source of getting into faith.

Those who choose to leave the faith of their fathers give themselves over to seducing spirits. That is the foundation of the New Age. They are spiritists and cultists because they deal with demon power. They pay large amounts of money to seek to know the future through some woman speaking with a man's voice out of her belly.

The "light" spoken of by these in New Age groups has only to do with deception. If you speak with New Age devotees, you will discover they do not believe in a personal god. They do not believe in heaven but think that heaven is here on earth.

They do not believe there is a hell where people burn. They believe that all people will see the "light" that they talk about and will finally come into peace with God and into heaven. Their idea of heaven is much different from that taught in the Bible.

One of the great deceptions of the devil is that all women and men will finally be saved and they will come into a place of tranquillity with God. The Bible very clearly teaches all of us that the way of the sinner is the way of death, and that the wages of sin is death.

There are two eternities. Jesus spoke very clearly of these.

In the best-selling book, *Embraced by the Light,* Betty Eadie writes that man isn't basically sinful, and that the "light" is love that draws us all into paradise.

Ms. Eadie failed, however, to look in the Bible and get the proper wording. The Bible says the devil comes deceiving people *as* "an angel of light" (2 Cor. 11:14). It doesn't say he *is* an angel of light.

The Bible makes it clear that Satan is a murderer and a liar. He is a deceiver who was from the beginning an evil one. There is no light in him, only darkness.

Anyone who follows Satan will end up where there is no light and that will be what the Bible calls eternal damnation — hell itself.

"I Don't Believe in Hell."

You may say, "I don't believe in hell."

Belief does not make anything true or false. I believe in eternity, immortality for the saints, and hell for sinners. However, that is not true because I believe it; it is true because the Bible says so.

You may not believe the sun will rise to-morrow, but that will not keep it from rising. At the same time, you may believe the sun *will* rise tomorrow, but your belief does not make it rise.

Before Columbus made his voyage to the new world, "scientists" believed the earth was flat and square, and theologians found "proof texts" so that they could agree with science — just as many do today concerning evolution. Their beliefs, however, did not make it true.

Your wishing or believing that there is no hell will not make it so or not so. Jesus himself talked more about hell than anyone else in the Bible. Not to believe in hell is not to believe in Jesus. If hell is something important enough for Him to talk about, then we need to understand all that the Bible tells us about it.

Life after Death

Jesus, in telling the story of the rich man Lazarus, gives us a unique view of life after death and of heaven and hell.

> And there was a certain beggar named Lazarus, which was laid at his gate, full of sores,
> And desiring to be fed with the crumbs which fell from the rich man's table: moreover the dogs came and licked his sores.

And it came to pass, that the beggar died, and was carried by the angels into Abraham's bosom: the rich man also died, and was buried;

And in hell he lift up his eyes, being in torments, and seeth Abraham afar off, and Lazarus in his bosom.

And he cried and said, Father Abraham, have mercy on me, and send Lazarus, that he may dip the tip of his finger in water, and cool my tongue; for I am tormented in this flame.

But Abraham said, Son, remember that thou in thy lifetime receivedst thy good things, and likewise Lazarus evil things: but now he is comforted, and thou art tormented.

And beside all this, between us and you there is a great gulf fixed: so that they which would pass from hence to you cannot; neither can they pass to us, that would come from thence.

Then he said, I pray thee therefore, father, that thou wouldest send him to my father's house:

For I have five brethren; that

he may testify unto them, lest they also come into this place of torment.

Abraham saith unto him, They have Moses and the prophets; let them hear them.

And he said, Nay, father Abraham: but if one went unto them from the dead, they will repent.

And he said unto him, If they hear not Moses and the prophets, neither will they be persuaded, though one rose from the dead (Luke 16:20-31).

This is one of the most terrifying stories of the Bible. Jesus did not relate this account of the rich man and Lazarus for our amusement, nor was He speaking a parable. This rich man at one time walked the earth, and Lazarus was an historical character. One man went to hell, the other to heaven.

The rich man who, like all of us, had a free will and a conscience apparently lived his life denying God and running from Him. Once dead, however, he remained conscious and aware of his surroundings. In fact, his memory and mind were still active, and he was able to see his loved ones still alive on the earth.

How horrible that must be for those who die without Christ.

All your screams and pleadings and bargaining will have no effect on your family's daily activities. You will scream and scream and see them walk through their daily routines — but, in time, they will join you in the place of torment unless they give their lives to Christ.

Like Lazarus, the believer in Jesus Christ receives eternal life because the Saviour has won the ultimate victory over death. By purchasing each soul with His own blood, Jesus gives freely the gift of life to those who believe in Him.

[1] Maurice Rawlings, *Beyond Death's Door* (New York, NY: Bantam Books, 1979), p. 29.
[2] Rawlings, *Beyond Death's Door.*

Chapter

4

Worshiping the
Dead

When I was in Moscow last year, I visited the tomb of Lenin, the man many Russians worshiped as a god. I went inside and viewed the body, which has been encased in glass for over 70 years. As I was looking at Lenin's body, I was told that one of his ears and his nose had disintegrated and that artificial ones had been put in their place. Some god.

Grant's tomb in New York City is one of many formal burial places in the world that denotes a person honored by his or her country. At the same time, this final resting place of former president and war hero Ulysses S. Grant speaks of the humiliation and utter disregard his fellow-man has for his memory.

In early 1995, private organizations were successful in finally removing graffiti, vandalism, and even human waste, from Grant's tomb — evidence that all men are equal in the final analysis.

To many people, Abraham Lincoln appears "larger than life" because of his impressive achievements. But this revered man still had to face physical death.

Did you know Abraham Lincoln's corpse has been exhumed twice? Why? Because people wanted to know if he was still there! Remnants of his body were in the ground, of course, but the man himself had long ago gone to his eternal dwelling.

Why do people worship the dead instead of the living God? Because Satan has deceived them.

What does the Bible say about the dead? It says all men die *once*, not many times. There is no murky language here. Once.

God teaches us implicitly that each person dies one physical death. Therefore, to worship a dead man or woman or child is folly because they cannot respond to your worship in any way.

We have discussed the numerous ways that people try to contact the dead, but what about the actual worshiping of a deceased person?

Millions of people around the world worship the spirits of the dead. All Buddhists pray to the spirits of the dead, burning incense and candles as part of their worship.

Even Americans worship their dead heroes.

> • The evolutionists still worship Darwin. He's been dead many years, but his false theories are read and studied as if they were sacred writings.
> • Each year thousands of people visit the home of Elvis Presley in Memphis, Tennessee. His grave is laden with flowers, messages, and trinkets placed there by fans of the singer who died in 1977. Nearly 20 years after his death, Elvis is still worshiped by fans who celebrate his birthday as if he were a president.
> • Another dead musician, Jim Morrison, who died of a drug-induced heart attack in 1971, is still worshiped today. His grave in Paris is littered with notes and flowers. Kids have even committed suicide there as an act of worship.

Ancient civilizations continually presented

sacrifices to the dead, and we consider them primitive and uncivilized. And yet, Americans do the same today in the sense that money and relationships are sacrificed in order to worship someone who has already gone to the other side.

Dragged into Eternity

One of my closest encounters with the worship of death began with a former witch doctor in Brazil.

Orlando had the unfortunate experience of being baptized to the devil before he was born. Just a few hours before his birth, the blood from a slain chicken was poured on the belly of Orlando's mother. A witch doctor chanted all kinds of strange words and rubbed the blood on this woman.

Orlando became a remarkable witch doctor. Even at two years of age, under the power of the devil, he could write prescriptions — in Latin. People would fill them and claim healing.

Orlando's brother, a boy about 12, had also been taught witchcraft. The boy was so tormented, however, that he almost lost his mind.

When Orlando would ask him what was wrong, the boy would reply, "Two devils are fighting to see which one would get my soul."

Orlando, however, didn't take any of this very seriously.

After a time, the brother became violently

sick. One day Orlando was the only other person in the room as he watched his brother writhe in pain from a high fever.

Suddenly, Orlando's spiritual eyes were opened, and he could see two huge demons hovering over the boy. They grabbed at his brother, choked him, pulled him, as the boy screamed for help. This battle continued, until the two demons pulled him out the window.

At that moment, Orlando's natural eyesight came back to him, and he saw the face of his brother staring in horror. He was dead.

These two demonic spirits fought for control over his brother's life, then dragged him off into eternity.

After I met Orlando, I took him all over Brazil, then to the United States. Everywhere he went, he told this story.

Similar instances are not uncommon in societies and cultures that think they can play with the devil. Worshipping evil and death produces evil and death.

Communicating with the Dead

Most pagan religions teach that it is possible to reach across the chasm of death and talk to people who once lived upon this earth.

Hinduism, India's most prevalent religion, teaches that communication with the dead is possible. As a result, these poor people make all kinds of idols to the dead and worship them. They take incense and candles and flowers and food and put it before a pagan temple, trying to reach over to the other side.

Deceived by demon power, they are taught that these dead idols can answer their prayers and help them through the struggles of life. Unfortunately, the troubles of these worshipers only increase as demons are given control over their lives.

In China, through Buddhism and Confucianism and other religions, people are taught there is a possibility of talking with the dead.

These worshipers hear strange little voices and say, "Yes, yes, I think that's him." They *feel* they are communicating with the dead, when in actuality, it is the demon spirits they are reaching.

Such religious activity is a direct violation of the warnings of God Almighty.

> And the soul that turneth after such as have familiar spirits, and after wizards, to go a whoring after them, I will even set my face against that soul, and will cut him off from among his people (Lev. 20:6).

Spirit communication, however, is not

confined to the East. Our Western civilizations engage in the same kind of dangerous activity.

Bound by Spiritism

When I was in England many years ago, I met the daughter of Charles Hadden Spurgeon, the great nineteenth-century preacher. He had been dead 50 years or more by this time.

Spurgeon's daughter attended a Methodist church but told me she was greatly disturbed. "For many years, I have been trying to reach my father, and I have gotten so deeply into spiritism that I don't know how to get out," she told me one evening.

Her pastor had suggested she come and talk with me about this problem. Although I didn't know her family, I surmised that she was telling the truth. She was so distraught and haggard from her futile conversations with spirits that she looked like a witch.

After praying the sinner's prayer with her, I placed my hand on her stomach and with a strong voice said, "You spirit of divination, come out of her! COME OUT OF HER!"

Suddenly, she said, "Something has happened. The power is broken inside; I am now free!"

She left that place completely free for the first time in her life since getting involved in spiritism.

Many older civilizations heap their teaching upon generation after generation. This is particularly true in eastern Europe, where it is felt that hordes of demons roam the wilderness at night.

Many people gather at cemeteries and stand in front of the tombs for hours at a time, eating, burning incense, and trying to communicate with the dead. It has been a custom among the wealthy to build a small room in front of the tombs, where grieving families stay for long periods of time to try and contact the deceased loved one.

In London, there are reports of spirits roaming about in and around the Tower of London.

In Normandy, where literally thousands have died in wars and purgings, demons have taken up residence in places where the murdered died, cursing and blaspheming. The devil loves these kinds of places.

Visits from the Dead?

Many people today relate stories about their loved ones coming back to visit them on earth. Is that possible?

Death is a finality of life. Death is the great separator that divides a person from time to eternity. People who die cannot come back and have communication with those who are alive. Spiritism carries this mystery on, generation after generation. It is a complete lie, and the function and operation of a demon.

Because I am human, I have thought before that communication with a departed loved one would be good. But the Word of God teaches us that the dead go to two places: everlasting life or everlasting death. Therefore, they have no communication with people living on earth. Always keep in mind the story of the rich man and Lazarus. The rich man was desperate to get word to his family on earth.

Although the Word of God teaches us of the everlasting abodes of humans, God forbids us to try and communicate with the dead.

I once knew a fine Christian lady who outlived all her family by many years. Even her son passed away a decade before his mother.

Thelma's whole life revolved around her family, especially the men. When her brother, father, husband, and finally son, all departed, she was left with only memories. She lived in the past.

After her funeral, friends were mingling in her home, when one noticed unusual-looking cards stuffed inside a tea cup. Looking further, it was revealed that this dear lady had consulted a medium in an attempt to communicate with her deceased family members.

What terrible deception! The Bible warns against communicating with spirits. It is forbidden.

There shall not be found among you any one that maketh his son or his daughter to pass through the fire, or that useth divination, or an observer of times, or an enchanter, or a witch,

Or a charmer, or a consulter with familiar spirits, or a wizard, or a necromancer.

For all that do these things are an abomination unto the Lord: and because of these abominations the Lord thy God doth drive them out from before thee (Deut. 18:10-12).

Houdini thought he had the power to reach back into this world again. He told his disciples: Be listening because I will be talking to you. But after these many, many years, Houdini has not one time communicated with anybody on this side of death, which is the side of life.

The Bible is a true book, and we do not move back and forth with information. We walk in God and in truth and in light.

Talking with the Devil

Mortal man, for 6,000 years, has sought information about life after death.

In ancient Babylon, men communicated with pagan gods — demons masquerading as plant gods, sun gods, mountain gods — and attempted to penetrate this curtain of death. As we discussed earlier, the Egyptians were very much interested in the mystery of death. Royalty spent lifetimes preparing for the afterlife.

King Saul of Israel sought to cross the bridge of death to secure information.

> Then said Saul unto his servants, Seek me a woman that hath a familiar spirit, that I may go to her, and inquire of her. And his servants said to him, Behold, there is a woman that hath a familiar spirit at Endor (1 Sam. 28:7).

This historical character, King Saul, had drifted so far away from God that he could no longer communicate with Him. Saul sought information about the future, and turned to a witch to do it.

> And Saul disguised himself, and put on other raiment, and he went, and two men with him, and they came to the woman by night: and he said, I pray thee, divine unto me by the familiar spirit, and bring me him up, whom I shall name unto thee (1 Sam. 28:8).

Anyone who searches the hidden secrets of death will be deceived by the devil, who is the predator of the night and darkness.

Sometime after the turn of the century, Thomas Edison spent considerable time trying to invent a machine to talk with the dead. Encyclopedias tell us that Edison was never a religious man but a believer in a "higher power," which is much different from the more effective and correct term, Creator.

The world-famous inventor spoke to newspaper reporters fairly often about his search for spirit communication, but it is said no such machine or evidence for one exists. That isn't quite so.

In his 1920 book, *My Life and Other Sundry Experiences*, Edison devoted several pages to both his thoughts on the afterlife and his invention. He writes that he was working closely with an associate who suddenly died. After this, there is no mention of the machine by Edison. We can speculate that he "tried it out" on his recently-departed assistant and found the machine to be ineffective.

If someone of renown and intelligence dabbles in this kind of experimentation, what does that say about mankind's spiritual state? People of Edison's day were somewhat desensitized to spirit communication, however, since seances and mediums enjoyed wide popularity. Communicating with the dead, however, is nothing more than talking with the devil.

Chapter
5

Searching for Immortality

Immortality is one of the most debated —
and controversial — subjects of our time.

- Buddhists teach that through
reincarnation the human soul lives
after human death.
- Hindus teach that man in his
next life can take on the form of
animal life or even insect life.
- Communists teach that man
is not immortal and has no future.
- Infidels teach that man is not
immortal and has no Creator.

- Rationalists teach that man has no proof of immortality.
- Evolutionists teach that man evolved from an amoeba and will continue to evolve.
- Humanists teach that man is his own creator and god.
- Philosophers teach that man is confined to wandering in mental darkness without hope.

What is the truth about the eternalness of man? Let us probe into this mystery of immortality.

Thanatology — The Science of Death

The term for the study of the medical, psychological, and social problems associated with death and dying is thanatology. Taken from the Greek word for "death," it does not study life after death. To study the hereafter, you must move into religion or theology, and that is not a "science" in the world's terms; it is a belief system.

Thanatology, a recently discovered subject, has surprisingly become popular with university students in America. Although the "experts" considered death a morbid subject that should be avoided, college classes on the subject were quickly filled by inquisitive students.

You don't have to attend college, however, to study death. In the jungles of Asia and on the streets of America, I have seen people dabbling in the science of death. These scenes weren't in a laboratory or university, but when fortune tellers and witch doctors attract crowds fascinated with immortality, it is the study of death just the same.

As we have seen from brief glimpses into other cultures and history, man has always searched for truth concerning the hereafter. I've seen evidences of this many times in my ministry. In fact, man's greatest explorations have been in the search for immortality — the desire to live forever.

Whether you study the beliefs of the American Indians, the ancient people of India, the oral cultures of Africa, or the myths and legends of the Eskimo, you will find one predominant theme — where man came from and where he is going after physical death.

Every intelligent person thinks of death. I have heard people say they don't give it a thought. Don't believe it.

Man — A Temporary Visitor

Poetry, drama, literature, music, and art have been the vehicles through which man has expressed this desire and longing for eternal life and immortality — to live forever without death.

In many ways the arts have more accurately expressed the fact that life goes on and on, rather than the interminable philosophical discussions, the vain speculations and theories, and the search for a "science" of death.

A science is "systematized knowledge derived from observation, study, and experimentation carried on in order to determine the nature or principles of what is being studied." Science is expected to be the study of proven facts.

The science of death can study *why* men die — all of the diseases and conditions that result in death — and *how* people die, but there are no "facts" able to be tested in a laboratory about the afterlife.

Science is not supposed to be built on someone's experience, yet — if the Bible is discounted — all that is left are the experiences of those who report having after-death experiences. And those experiences are not objective. They are subjective, having taken place when the body was lying inert and sometimes lifeless on earth.

Some "scientific" facts about man's attitude to death and the afterlife can be proven. Here are a few:

> • Man is the only creature not entirely satisfied with the life he lives on the face of the earth — as we can see throughout history.

• Man is the only earth creature who actually yearns for life beyond this earth.

• Man has an inherent knowledge that there is something beyond this life.

Today, however, man is consistently looking for answers in all the wrong places. Why? Because men do not want to acknowledge a Creator. Why? If they do, they must also accept the fact that they are accountable to God — and that implies a coming judgment.

The bottom-line truth is that, after Adam and Eve, mankind became temporary visitors for the return to our permanent home — eternity.

In spite of man's rejection of God's Word, it is in the Bible that we find a number of facts about the afterlife, which are "scientific" proof to a Christian. Let's look at some of these facts.

Deathless

That "homing" device in man triggers that age-old question best expressed in the words of Job, the oldest book in the Bible: "If a man die, shall he live again?" (Job 14:14).

Job found his answer:

For I know that my redeemer liveth, and that he shall stand at the

latter day upon the earth:
And though after my skin
worms destroy this body, yet in my
flesh [his new spiritual body] shall
I see God (Job 19:25-26).

Job, after enduring terrible hardships, was
one of the first men to study death. Science, after all, is a search for knowledge. Job's suffer-
ings drove him to understand the science of death.
Many intellectuals have wrestled with the study
of death for years, yet all they had to do was
read Job 19.

Only the gospel of Christ brings truth about
eternal life and how to gain immortality. The
word "immortality" involves life, and those who
go to hell experience the real death, the second
death — separation from God. So the unrigh-
teous dead live forever, but they are not immortal as God is immortal.

The apostle Paul wrote to Timothy:

But is now made manifest by
the appearing of our Saviour Jesus
Christ, who hath abolished death,
and hath brought life and immortality to light through the gospel (2
Tim. 1:10).

Only the good news of Jesus Christ brings

truth about immortality. In the textbooks of man, you cannot find the truth regarding man's eternal destiny.

The Bible is very specific and careful about the truth regarding life and death because all human life is eternal, existing without ever becoming nonexistent. We cannot say everyone is immortal, however. The exact meaning of the term, *immortal,* is "deathless," and only God is a true immortal. He had no beginning, and He has no end. There is no death in Him, and no time.

The Bible says Jesus *is* the beginning and the end (Rev. 1:11). Through Jesus, people can have immortality by being born again.

Christians do experience physical death. However, Christians really do not "die." They simply walk through the closing of one existence and the opening of another. You might say that, through Jesus, Christians *become* immortal. Once through this existence, they will never experience any kind of death again.

"Heavenly Places"

Eternity is a state of being, not a place, although locations and places will exist for us to live in eternity. In eternity, those immortal in God may live in heaven or on a restored earth or wherever else God makes "places" for us to live, work, and worship Him.

We will never understand life and death, however, if we think in terms of places — here and there. We must think in terms of here and everywhere. God is not confined to one place called heaven. He is omnipresent, which means everywhere.

We will not be "everywhere" at the same time in eternity any more than we can be on earth. We will exist forever as those who have become immortal, never to experience death again, but that existence will be in various places at various times as God wills.

As author Lambert Dolphin states:

> If the readers understand that the "heavenly places" are all around us, and not far beyond the reaches of space, then death is merely the lifting of a veil that separates the physical from the spiritual."[1]

It limits our thinking about eternity to talk of here and there as if heaven is only one place. Christians should focus on having eternal life, not on continuing to exist in one different location.

The Bible does not give us many details about the afterlife, only that it exists and that time limits and death are temporary measures.

Death to a Christian is to pass to the other

side of time. Death is a curtain through which we pass to a more abundant life. I am looking forward to it.

For Christians, death is stepping from darkness into light; for non-Christians, it is stepping from faint light into pitch darkness.

The English poet, John Keats, wrote a tragic poem, in which he lamented the fact he would soon die. The poem is full of despair about lost opportunities and relationships. If only he could have seen the glorious hope we have in Christ.

Death is stepping from winter into summer for Christians, from plainness and barrenness into glorious beauty, loveliness, and forever happiness and joy.

Truths about Eternity

A rich young ruler came to Jesus with the age-old question, "What must I do to obtain eternal life?"

> And, behold, one came and said unto him, Good Master, what good thing shall I do, that I may have eternal life?
> And he said unto him, Why callest thou me good? there is none good but one, that is, God: but if thou wilt enter into life, keep the commandments.

He saith unto him, Which? Jesus said, Thou shalt do no murder, Thou shalt not commit adultery, Thou shalt not steal, Thou shalt not bear false witness,

Honour thy father and thy mother: and, Thou shalt love thy neighbour as thyself.

The young man saith unto him, All these things have I kept from my youth up: what lack I yet?

Jesus said unto him, If thou wilt be perfect, go and sell that thou hast, and give to the poor, and thou shalt have treasure in heaven: and come and follow me.

But when the young man heard that saying, he went away sorrowful: for he had great possessions (Matt. 19:16-22).

As a wealthy Jew, this man must have been educated in Old Testament truths, so he knew that everyone exists eternally. He was really asking, "How can I live out eternity with God? How can I spend eternity in the light, not the darkness?"

Jesus had a simple answer, "Come and follow me."

To do that, the young man had to give up everything else. He refused to do that and went away feeling very sorrowful.

In this encounter, and also in Jesus' illustration of the rich man who built more barns and lost his soul, we get God's perspective on eternity:

> And he spake a parable unto them, saying, The ground of a certain rich man brought forth plentifully:
>
> And he thought within himself, saying, What shall I do, because I have no room where to bestow my fruits?
>
> And he said, This will I do: I will pull down my barns, and build greater; and there will I bestow all my fruits and my goods.
>
> And I will say to my soul, Soul, thou hast much goods laid up for many years; take thine ease, eat, drink, and be merry.
>
> But God said unto him, Thou fool, this night thy soul shall be required of thee: then whose shall those things be, which thou hast provided?
>
> So is he that layeth up treasure

for himself, and is not rich toward
God (Luke 12:16-21).

Let's look at the truths these passages teach
us about eternity:

- Eternity is simply a "label"
for the reality that life never ends.
- Eternity for the Christian includes possibly many places to ex-
plore and serve in, but for the non-
believer, eternity is centered in one
place: hell.
- Eternity means leaving everything that belongs to time behind
on earth. Nothing we have here can
go with us. Only what we are, what
we have become — good or bad —
accompanies us.

The rich, young ruler who held onto his
goods and the rich man who found his identity
in his wealth both left this world without anything. The beggar who went to Abraham's bosom, however, had more real wealth than the rich
man who lifted up his eyes in hell (Luke 16:22-
23).

- Eternity cannot be experienced in this earthly body, these

temples of clay in which we live now.
  • Eternity for the Christian is being in the presence of Christ.

What could be better than that?

Eternal Questions and Answers

The Bible answers many questions people have about the afterlife:
  • *Where will I spend eternity?* You will spend it in heaven or hell, whichever you have chosen through what you did with Jesus.

> For God so loved the world, that he gave his only begotten Son, that whosoever believeth in him should not perish, but have everlasting life (John 3:16).

  • *Will I be aware and conscious?* Yes, in hell or in eternity with God, you will be consciously aware of yourself and your surroundings. The rich man and the beggar both were acutely conscious of where they were and who they were.
  • *Will I recognize others, and can they recognize me in eternity? Will I look as I do now?* Yes, we will. "Now I know in part; but then shall I know even as also I am known" (1 Cor. 13:12).

You will look as you do now, yet not exactly the same because you will be transfigured, living in a perfect body without the blemishes and wrinkles the physical body develops.

> There are also celestial bodies, and bodies terrestrial: but the glory of the celestial is one, and the glory of the terrestrial is another (1 Cor. 15:40).

• *Will I be able to see what is real and then make a different choice than I did in this life?* No. Once you pass through the curtain of time through the door of death, your destiny is irrevocable, unchangeable, and fixed forever.

> And as it is appointed unto men once to die, but after this the judgment (Heb. 9:27).

• *What age will I be?* We have only "proof" in answer to this question. The Bible says we will be "like" Jesus, which probably means in the prime of life.

> And as we have borne the image of the earthy, we shall also bear the image of the heavenly (1 Cor. 15:49).

Someone has said everyone will look about 33, Jesus' age when He died and rose again. Others simply say that no matter the degree of maturity, we will not look old or aged. However, this is something not spelled out in Scripture.

What a glorious hope! No one will ever have to push a loved one in a wheelchair or spoon-feed the elderly or paralyzed. Those who grow old and tired, hurting and deformed on earth, will not be like that in heaven if they have accepted Jesus.

Eternal life will flow through us as it did through Adam before he sinned. We will have become immortal — deathless.

Jesus: Living Proof

The Lord Jesus Christ is the only one who can teach us about eternal life and immortality. He lived in eternity, then came to earth as a baby and lived in time. After that, He went back to eternity through the door of death — and returned to walk on earth in His eternal body for about 40 days.

Paul gave us the "scientific" facts about death:

> But now is Christ risen from
> the dead, and become the firstfruits
> of them that slept.
> For since by man came death,

by man came also the resurrection
of the dead.

For as in Adam all die, even so
in Christ shall all be made alive (1
Cor. 15:20-22).

Jesus is living, scientific, objective proof
that what the Bible tells us about life, death, and
life after death is true.

Thanatology should begin and end with the
Bible. Otherwise, it is not scientific at all but
merely vain speculation.

Before their deaths many people have promised to come back and talk with their friends and
relatives. Spiritists, occultists, and those involved
in angel worship claim to be able to talk to those
on the other side of death. Not one of these claims
or "returns" to earth, however, has been documented as real or been able to be submitted to
objective testing. All hinge on a mental belief.

On the other hand, the facts surrounding
Jesus' "return" from the dead are very well-
documented. Let's look at these documented
facts:

• Jesus rose from the dead and showed himself to be still alive by many "infallible proofs."

Until the day in which he was
taken up, after that he through the
Holy Ghost had given command-

ments unto the apostles whom he had chosen:

To whom also he shewed himself alive after his passion by many infallible proofs, being seen of them forty days, and speaking of the things pertaining to the kingdom of God (Acts 1:2-3).

• After He died, Jesus was seen by 500 men and women at one time and by smaller groups of people on other occasions (see John, chapters 20-21). The apostle Paul documents this fact:

After that, he was seen of above five hundred brethren at once; of whom the greater part remain unto this present, but some are fallen asleep (1 Cor.15:6).

• Jesus showed His disciples the scars on His body from the crucifixion, proving He was the same person who had died and that He now had a new living, breathing body. The body of an illusion or a "spirit" cannot be felt.

A week later his disciples were in the house again, and Thomas was with them. Though the doors were locked, Jesus came and stood among them and said, "Peace be with you!"

Then he said to Thomas, "Put your finger here; see my hands. Reach out your hand and put it into my side. Stop doubting and believe" (John 20:26-27;NIV).

• After the resurrection, Jesus had a "flesh and bones" body, proved by the fact that He could eat and digest food.

> Behold my hands and my feet, that it is I myself: handle me, and see; for a spirit hath not flesh and bones, as ye see me have.
>
> And when he had thus spoken, he shewed them his hands and his feet.
>
> And while they yet believed not for joy, and wondered, he said unto them, Have ye here any meat?
>
> And they gave him a piece of a broiled fish, and of an honeycomb.
>
> And he took it, and did eat before them (Luke 24:39-43).

• Jesus told His disciples He was going on ahead of them into eternity to prepare "mansions (places to live)" for them.

> In my Father's house are many
> mansions: if it were not so, I would
> have told you. I go to prepare a
> place for you.
> And if I go and prepare a place
> for you, I will come again, and re-
> ceive you unto myself; that where
> I am, there ye may be also (John
> 14:2-3).

These well-documented historical facts prove that Jesus is the only person who ever lived on this earth, died by public execution, and then appeared publicly to many people after He was raised from the dead. I would say that makes Jesus the "expert" on immortality and life after death.

The Corn Patch Sermon

When I was in London visiting the Egyptian section of the British Museum, I passed a large casket containing a mummy. Around the mummy were arranged some artifacts and some seeds of grain. At the foot of the coffin was a large can in which corn stalks, three or four feet high, were growing.

As I stood there with other visitors, the curator of the museum opened the casket for us.

Inside, we noticed the money of ancient times and the personal belongings of the man who had been mummified. He probably had died 1,000 to 1,500 years before Jesus was born.

"This is very interesting," the curator said. "We decided to see if the corn found in this tomb would still grow, so we planted several grains in this bucket and placed it under this skylight above us."

Pointing overhead, he said, "Through the skylight, the corn got sun, and we kept pouring a little water on it from time to time. Now look at it! Isn't it beautiful, and isn't it green?"

"Sir," I said, "this is the most thrilling thing I have ever seen in my life."

A little bit startled at my enthusiastic response, he asked, "Why?"

I responded, "Because if God loves corn like that, God loves me even more. If I am planted in the earth in a coffin, surely my body will come forth one day to live again."

The curator stared at me and did not answer. I do not suppose he had ever gotten a sermon from a corn patch before.

As I looked at that ancient corn growing just as fresh and beautiful as if it had come from a year-old seed, I saw resurrection! With my own eyes, I saw corn dead for thousands of years once again alive and producing.

If God can keep life in corn for perhaps

3,500 years and then bring it forth when it is planted, He can do the same for us.

When I preach funerals and observe the beautiful flowers around me, I usually say, "Dear beloved ones, do you think God loves these flowers more than He does this loved one who is being laid to rest? See these flowers before us? By tomorrow, they will be wilting, and perhaps by the next day, they will be dead.

"But plant the seeds or the bulbs from those flowers again, and they will 'come forth from the dead.' They will bloom again with a new loveliness, a new freshness, and a new fragrance. Now do you really think God loves flowers more than He does a human being?"

Jesus pointed out that if something is not planted and dies, nothing grows out of it.

I tell you the truth, unless a kernel of wheat falls to the ground and dies, it remains only a single seed. But if it dies, it produces many seeds (John 12:24;NIV).

Jesus was "planted" in death and rose again, making a way for us to follow in His pattern.

Jesus answered, "I am the way and the truth and the life. No one comes to the Father except through me (John 14:6;NIV).

We will be planted in death, but unlike the flowers, we never cease to exist. We continue to exist in heaven or hell until the "resurrection of the dead," when the bodies of believers will also rise again as bodies that are not subject to death.

> So when this corruptible shall have put on incorruption, and this mortal shall have put on immortality, then shall be brought to pass the saying that is written, Death is swallowed up in victory (1 Cor. 15:54).

Immortality is beautiful! We will have eternal life flowing through us as Adam had before he sinned.

[1] Lambert Dolphin, *Jesus: Lord of Time and Space* (Green Forest, AR: New Leaf Press, 1988).

Chapter
6

In Those Final Moments

Consider for a moment the contrast between the way people are born and how people die.

Birth has always fascinated mankind. In the first moments of life — when a baby comes into this world — the tiny infant is the center of attention.

The doctor gazes at it.

The mother and father are excited and happy. "Does he have both legs? Does he have five toes on each foot? Is everything all right?"

It is a very joyful and happy moment.

The first 30 minutes of man's existence on this earth is a miracle of miracles.

He comes forth from his mother's body, the doctor cuts the cord separating him from his mother, and he becomes a separate unit for the rest of his life.

The doctor is very alert as he checks the baby's breathing and examines every inch of the tiny body.

Those first few minutes are crucial ones of destiny. The parents give this human person a name, and he becomes one of the citizens of his community — and of this world.

Right from the beginning, a baby has a guardian angel who continually sees the face of the Father.

> Take heed that ye despise not one of these little ones; for I say unto you, That in heaven their angels do always behold the face of my Father which is in heaven (Matt. 18:10).

God is, therefore, close to each child, always watching over His precious little one.

After birth, this human person goes through a series of interesting events of growing, learning, living, and loving. He is an immortal soul who is morally responsible for his actions and thinking. There are multitudes of activities and decisions he must make before he reaches the final 30 minutes of his life.

Poppies in the Coffin

Americans, it has been said, are in denial about death and refuse to think about it. This estrangement could, in part, be due to the fact that death is foreign to most Americans.

Most people die in sterile hospitals where they are cared for by nurses and doctors and away from direct contact with family members. Then the body is taken by hearse to a funeral home where professional undertakers prepare the body for burial.

In Third World countries, however, people touch death every day. They see it and smell it and feel it.

Most loved ones in more primitive cultures suffer and die within their own thatched-roof huts, where they have been cared for by family members. Even if they have been hospitalized, relatives are often responsible for providing food and taking care of the sick person's physical needs.

When death comes, the body is bathed and clothed by family members who then often carry it in a wooden coffin outside the town for burial.

Death is a part of their lives. That may be why certain societies have elaborate death preparations.

Years ago, while doing missionary work in

Tibet, my companions and I often had to sleep in barn lofts with animals kept on the floor below us.

One night, right beside me in the loft was a large wooden and painted Chinese coffin along with millions of decorative opium poppies.

After undressing, I laid my clothes on the empty coffin and smelled the sweet fragrance of the opium poppies all night.

The next morning I asked the owner of the horse barn inn, "Why is the coffin in the loft?"

He said, "Oh, that is mine. I know I shall die and I want my coffin to look as I desired, so I had it made in preparation of my death."

Unlike this pragmatic approach to death, others are more concerned with what they leave behind.

Leaving a Legacy

Meyer Amschel Rothschild founded a bank in Frankfurt. He knew that his moment had come to leave this world. Calling his five sons into his bedroom, the elder Rothschild said, "My sons, leave this place."

Pointing to one son he said, "You go to London and become involved in banking and in the stock market. You can rule the country through finance."

He pointed to another son and said, "Go to Paris, open banks and deal exclusively with banking, and you can control that country."

He pointed to the third son and said, "You go to Vienna and be a banker. The world is controlled by money."

Another was dispatched with similar instructions to Naples. The oldest son remained with the bank in Frankfurt.

In those dying moments, the old father Rothschild literally changed the future of the world. The importance of this father's responsible action was far-reaching.

Although several generations have passed since that day, it is not inaccurate to say that the Rothschilds saved the British Empire. When it was thought the English had lost the war to Napoleon, the Rothschild brothers all agreed that no money would be loaned to Napoleon for war but that Great Britain could have any amount needed.

History records that Wellington defeated Napoleon at Waterloo.

The Bible records that when Isaac was ready to pass away, he wished to bless his two sons, Esau and Jacob.

Years later, when Jacob knew it was time for him to die, he called all of his sons into his tent and gave them their future, strength, power, and place in history. As he lay dying, he told all 12 boys what their destinies would be. When he finished, he died (Gen. 48-50).

Although my goal has always been to build a team ministry with my three sons, I knew that would require me to give away some control and authority. Today, however, they have assumed much of the administrative duties of the ministry, and I know that when the Lord calls me home, it will continue and not miss a beat.

Do you attempt to put off death by refusing to make a will or talk to those who can assume control of your financial affairs? You're not cheating or delaying death, really. You are simply not facing up to an inevitability.

Less Than 24 Hours

For some reason, a preacher who lived in Indianapolis hated our Christian TV station and often criticized me to others. When he got cancer, however, his son and wife told me the man spent all his time calling up people he had mistreated and asking for forgiveness.

While I was attending a camp meeting, this man was brought in an ambulance to see me. After being rolled inside, he began to cry and say, "I have to ask you, Pastor Sumrall, to forgive me. I've said bad things about you. I didn't want to die until I had your forgiveness."

At that moment, Kenneth Copeland passed by the door. I said, "Brother Copeland, come in here. This man is dying of cancer, and he's a pastor. Would you pray for him?"

We laid hands on the man and very tenderly prayed a sweet little prayer over him. Then I told him, "You are forgiven dear brother, completely. You'll be happy to know, I didn't know anything about this matter. Nobody told me. I stay so busy that I don't see anybody except the people I preach for."

"But you don't know how many terrible things I've said about you," he said, weeping.

"Please, brother," I said, "feel forgiven in Jesus' name."

The next day I heard he was dead. At the time he came to visit me, I'm sure he had not realized he had less than 24 hours to make things right.

When the Spirit Leaves the Body

When I was in Sweden, I stood by the bed of a Christian man. As his life left the body, I put my hands on his feet, his belly, the chest, and the head. The belly was the last place to become cold. Why? Because the belly is the seat and throne of the spirit of man.

The Lord Jesus said, "Out of his belly shall flow rivers of living water" (John 7:38).

The spirit of man, directed by the entire personality, includes the mind, the senses, and the will. At the time of death, the spirit releases faculties from the human body.

Your salvation is not primarily located in

your mind. It is in that born-again experience given by God at your salvation. Because the mind is part of the human soul, mind, emotions, and will, it is not the originator of dynamic truth. This is done in the spiritual man. A special contact and relationship with God is through the new birth.

The apostle Paul wrote, "You hath he quickened, who were dead in trespasses and sins" (Eph. 2:1).

In South Bend, Indiana, when a retired pastor, Reverend Peterson, went to be with the Lord, I was the only person in the room. As he was leaving the earth, this dear man spoke softly and distinctly said, "It's so beautiful, so beautiful, so satisfying."

He talked of the light as so bright, so beautiful. And then he entered into eternity.

As I touched his body, I noticed that his stomach was the last part to become cold.

In Indianapolis, Indiana, four of my close Christian friends and a young boy died in an airplane accident. One was about 50 years old, two of the men were maybe 35, and the fourth was a father who died along with his 12-year-old son.

The moment I heard about this tragedy, I went on my face before God. As I prayed, in my spirit I saw the five men.

With my spiritual eye, I saw them dressed in white hovering some 20 feet above the wreckage and looking down at their mangled bodies in the wreckage. In their resurrected bodies, however, all five of them were beautiful and happy.

One of them spoke. "Isn't this a mess?" he said.

Then I saw them move toward heaven as a group.

Funerals — For the Living

When I think of funerals, the one that comes to mind is that of Moses.

This great patriarch was gifted with a burial by God himself. After he had been granted the chance to view the Promised Land from a distance Moses died, and the Bible says God took care of the burial (Deut. 34:5-8).

The devil fought for the remains of Moses, and the angel Michael came to wrest him away. For 30 days, the children of Israel mourned Moses' death.

When Jacob, the patriarch of Israel, died in Egypt, the mourning for him lasted through 40 days of embalming the body for burial, 70 days of mourning, the days it took for his family and all of the Egyptian officials to travel back to the Cave of Machpelah in Canaan, and then 7 more days of mourning (Gen. 50:3-14).

From the beginning of time, respect and appreciation has been given to those who die. Ancient empires had funeral ceremonies that lasted a year. Most of these developed not only from a desire to comfort those still living but, somehow, to express a protest against death itself.

In cultures that did not have the Bible, death seemed unaccountable. Because of that inherent awareness that life really does not ever end, all peoples have treated death as basically unnatural. Funerals are ways in which people try to come to terms with the fact of death. It is popular today to say that funerals are for the benefit of the living.

Pagan Funerals

During our evangelistic and missionary days, our family lived extensively in pagan countries. In China and other Far East countries, we saw feasts for the dead, and ceremonies featuring flowers, bands of musicians, prayers by the priests, and so forth.

In China, I saw funerals that lasted for a week or 10 days. When the family could not mourn as sufficiently as they thought needful, they hired special mourners to weep for them. These professional mourners looked in the depths of grief, mourning with tears and saliva running down their faces.

In Communist countries funerals are especially sad because there is no hope of the hereafter and no belief in possible immortality.

I will never forget a funeral I witnessed in India — the funeral of a cow! There was great pomp, ceremony, dancing, and even mourners falling prostrate on the ground, foaming at the mouth. In a country that believes not only in reincarnation but in transmigration of souls (people coming back as animals), they believe that this dead cow might be one of their ancestors.

These ideas were developed long after the flood and in the times of Abraham and the time the children of Israel were in Egypt. The devil takes full control of the minds of people, until the Hindus now have over 100 million deities. It is possible that the sacred cow of Egypt and India, which is one of their deities, developed during the same centuries.

The apostle Paul wrote that Christians do not mourn as others who have no hope (1 Thess. 4:13). The common denominator in all the pagan funerals I have witnessed is hopelessness. The mourners I saw had no hope for eternity.

In a society like India's, death is a constant source of sadness because of the hopelessness. An Indian mother will tell you, "I've had 15 children; 13 are dead." Then she'll point to the two survivors. If the 13 were young enough, they are with the Lord in heaven. The mother may have 2, but God's got 13.

In all cultures and ways of dealing with the

dead, past and present funeral practices achieve three purposes:

1. Survivors are somehow pro-tected by these rituals from contact with death.
2. The dead person is initiated into his new life.
3. The dead person is given "safe conduct" to his new abode.

In Ireland, and even in the old days in this country, people held "wakes," at which family members and friends sat up awake all night with the dead person until the body was buried. Wakes also included feasts of food and drink brought in by neighbors and other family members.

In Christianity, however, funerals are gen-erally seen as a way of providing comfort and compassion for the family and friends left be-hind. Christians understand that funerals do noth-ing for the dead, only the living.

What about Cremation?

In India, there are funerals but no burials. Bodies usually are burned on funeral pyres.

Before British rule, widows were burned alive with their husbands' bodies. This practice was banned in recent years. Some other tribal customs are even more extreme or outrageous.

As far as I can see, the burning of corpses is actually a way of offering them up to Satan. Pagans worship fire as a god, and when they burn bodies, they are offering them to the god of fire. That is why I do not ever advise cremation.

The body is not sacred, and in the Resurrection it will not matter if the body is alive, ashes, dust, or dissolved in sea water. God can give us new bodies regardless of the state of the old ones. The precedent of pagan customs shows, however, that bodies are burned as satanic rituals.

Biblical precedents and Christian traditions based on the Bible stipulate burying the bodies of deceased loved ones and friends with respect.

Funerals — Big Business

Funerals are big business in the United States.

In recent years, the state of Indiana has had the highest national average spent per funeral — more than $6,000 each, counting cemetery spaces and markers.

It is very easy for grief-stricken relatives to go overboard in arranging funerals. Some are concerned that unless they purchase the most expensive coffin they will look "cheap" to those attending. Some relatives try to get rid of "guilt" feelings toward the deceased by paying for an elaborate funeral.

Too much importance is placed on funerals. Some funerals are spectacles while others are tasteful. Some funerals bring comfort to the mourners; others leave everyone attending feeling "empty." Some funerals are genuine celebrations; others are a mockery with the speaker unable to say one good thing about the deceased.

The funeral most remembered by those over 40 is probably that of President John F. Kennedy, which was televised nationwide. The nation mourned for days over the loss of their young president killed unexpectedly by an assassin.

I happened to be in Dallas when Kennedy was killed. By television I saw him walk out of his hotel in Fort Worth, greet a number of people, and get into his limousine and then go to his plane. He only went over to Dallas and during the flight we only received radio signals or comments, and upon his arrival in Dallas there were many people to greet him. I understand that several of his friends requested that he put the bulletproof top over his limousine; but he wanted to stand up to wave at the poeple and wanted them to have a good sight of him. One of the most shocking moments of my life was when a television reporter said, "My God! The president has been shot!" I saw his car whirl out of the caravan and head toward the hospital.

Recently, the funeral of President Richard Nixon brought an overwhelming outpouring of compassion from across the country and around the world. The media, who had ridiculed this great statesman for years, was shocked at the obvious respect that many Americans had for this former president.

The first funeral I remember was that of my little brother Archie who died of spinal meningitis just before his second birthday. At the time, I was about seven years old.

The second funeral I attended was that of my 87-year-old grandfather, a veteran of the Civil War, who was buried in his military uniform.

Down through history, there have been two kinds of funerals: those with some type of ceremony, and those in which the deceased is forgotten, sometimes even to the point of being buried in unknown graves.

The Bible tells of those killed in battle, some righteous and some wicked, who died without funerals.

Jehoiakim, one of the last kings of Judah, was buried without a funeral. He was cursed by God to be "buried with the burial of an ass" and have no one lamenting for him, because of his covetousness and his shedding of innocent blood (Jer. 22:18-19).

The Christian Funeral

Is a funeral necessary? Of course not.
Funerals are to make it easier for the living

to accept the fact that a loved one has gone beyond their reach. Funerals are to make it easier to let go of one who has died. Without the ritual of a funeral and burial, it seems harder to accept that someone is truly gone.

How many families have doubly grieved over a fallen young man or woman in time of war? Anguished by the death itself, they must also grieve over their lost chance to say goodbye with a funeral.

Thousands of American soldiers are buried on foreign soil. Many families of MIAs and POWs, whose remains have not yet been returned from the Vietnam war, still have not been able to put their grief behind them.

Funerals are to "pay last respects" to one who has passed through the curtain of time and the door of death.

Funerals for Christians should be home-going celebrations that reflect the character and personality of the deceased loved one. The Lord should be involved in the process. Family members operating in the peace of the Holy Spirit will know how much to spend and what kind of arrangements to make.

A story is told of a Greek named Aristeides trying to explain Christianity to a friend in the second century after Christ. He wrote:

If any righteous man among

the Christians passes from this
world, they rejoice and offer thanks
to God, and they escort his body
with songs and thanksgiving as if
he were setting out from one place
to another nearby.[1]

Christians of a certain African tribe are said
to exclaim joyfully upon the death of another
Christian, "He has arrived!" not "He has departed."

If we separated deaths from funerals, would
we see death any clearer?

Do funerals help us cope better with death?
Most people think so.

Gladys Hunt, the author of an old book, *The
Christian Way of Death,* wrote:

We are limited by concepts of
time and space; we need an eternal
point of view.[2]

Your reaction to death will be conditioned
by your reaction to God. Those afraid of God
are most fearful of death. Those who know Him
well, however, seem to welcome the opportunity of being with Him. That's the dimension
that transforms death — knowing God.

1 Tan, Paul Lee, *Encyclopedia of 7700 Illustrations* (Rockville, IL: Assurance Publishers, 1979), #1025, p. 309.
2 Hunt, Gladys M., *The Christian Way of Death*, reprinted as *Don't Be Afraid To Die* (Grand Rapids, MI: Zondervan Publishing Company, 1971).

Chapter
7

Death by Suicide

A teenager who drives 90 miles per hour around a dangerous curve certainly isn't in love with life. A man who is told by his doctor that another drop of alcohol will kill him, and continues to drink, has no respect for his body or his life.

To die by suicide is to die the death of a fool. Although few people will admit it, many recklessly flirt with suicide.

I am reminded of the man who had much professional success in the world and all the outward signs of happiness, but he was miserable. Job pressures and family problems left him heavily depressed. He had a heart condition and settled on an ingenious method for committing suicide — exercise himself to death.

Pushing his jogging regimen to the limit, this man one night had a heart attack while running through a park. *Great,* he thought *I'll pass on, and everyone will be better off.* But God did a strange thing as He looked down on this man: He let him live.

Rising to his feet and clutching at the pain in his chest, this man went home. Still not understanding the reprieve he'd been given, he tried the same thing the next night. Same result. Eventually, his exercise methods strengthened his heart muscle and with his health problems behind him, life became sweet.

All of us have to make a choice. Will we serve God or not serve God? We need to walk so carefully before our Creator that whether we live or die, we do it in a way that is pleasing to God.

The Rush to Self-Destruction

The fifth commandment charges, "Thou shalt not kill" (Exod. 20:13). Man, however, has devised many ways and different forms of killing his fellow man — and himself.

Killing has many forms:

- Genocide: to kill a race or nationality.
- Homicide: one man or woman kills another man or woman.

- Patricide: a son or daughter kills his or her father.
- Fratricide: to kill a brother or a sister.
- Infanticide: to kill a baby.
- Aborticide or feticide: to kill a pre-born baby — abortion.
- Suicide: to kill oneself.

It is this last definition that concerns us in this chapter. Suicide is a form of murder in which an individual takes his own life.

> Some physicians call suicide a disease.
> The law calls suicide a crime.
> Religion calls it a sin.
> The Japanese glorify it.
> The Israelites abhor it.
> Ancient Rome condoned it.

These are violent times in which we live. There is more violence per capita on the earth today than history has ever recorded.

Man's main problem is not worldwide devastation caused by famine, ethnic cleansing, or Communist domination as in Somalia, Bosnia, and China. Far more critical is the daily destruction of life from violent human relationships.

Self-destruction is part of this widespread violence. It is growing phenomenally with over

50,000 suicides annually in the United States.

At a meeting of doctors in San Francisco, it was revealed that medical officials speculate millions of humans now living are considering taking their own lives. The Associated Press reports over 200,000 Americans attempt suicide each year — one every 2-1/2 minutes.

Suicide has become the number 10 cause of death in the United States. It is the number *one* cause of death for those under 30. Statistics show more women than men commit suicide. The highest rates are among the middle and upper classes.

Twenty years ago, it was thought that our rapidly-increasing technology would bring a sort of Utopian society to fruition. Work weeks would decrease, and we would all have so much leisure time we wouldn't know what to do with it. Instead, people are more harried today than ever. They are literally collapsing under the weight of terrible pressures.

Our minds were not made to deal with the swirling problems we face today. In desperation, worried parents and children take what they think is an easy way out.

Death, however, is a threshold we cannot re-cross. It is final.

Suicide in the Bible

It is my belief that suicide is a fairly recent

phenomenon. The Bible includes the accounts of hundreds of people and records only three who committed suicide — and all had a cloud of gloom over them.

• *King Saul* — This once-mighty king of Israel lost the respect of the people. He lost a battle and eventually lost his throne and life.

> Then said Saul unto his armourbearer, Draw thy sword, and thrust me through . . . But his armourbearer would not. . . . Therefore Saul took a sword, and fell upon it (1 Sam. 31:4).

• *Ahithophel* — This traitor, who had once been David's counselor, suffered from shame, guilt, alienation, feelings of hopelessness, failure, depression, distress, and disappointment in love.

> And when Ahithophel saw that his counsel was not followed . . . gat him home to his house, to his city, and put his household in order, and hanged himself (2 Sam. 17:23).

• *Judas* — The most infamous suicide in history resulted from the greatest betrayal of all time.

> Then one of the twelve, called Judas Iscariot, went unto the chief priests, And said unto them, What will ye give me, and I will deliver him unto you? And they covenanted with him for thirty pieces of silver. . . . And he cast down the pieces of silver in the temple, and departed, and went and hanged himself (Matt. 26:14-15; 27:5).

I well remember the suicides of 1929, when the stock market crashed, and devastated investors jumped out of high-rise buildings to their deaths. Why? They were afraid to face life without any money in the bank.

Jesus predicted that in the last days men's hearts would fail them in fear.

> Men's hearts failing them for fear, and for looking after those things which are coming on the earth: for the powers of heaven shall be shaken (Luke 21:26).

If men and women could realize that their condition is prophetic, they would fight harder to be free.

Guarding against Suicidal Tendencies

The strongest instinct in human nature is

self-preservation. For a human to break that power and destroy his life means that he has rebelled against the strongest instinct given by God. Such a person is no longer normal.

If a person is not in his or her right mind — if a person is mentally impaired, God does not hold that person responsible for a rash decision. It is the same as a person who does not have the mental ability to consider a decision for Christ. Most people who commit suicide, however, know exactly what they are doing.

All of us need to guard against this pervasive spirit of suicide that is sweeping across the world. Here are some ways to protect yourself and your children:

• *Teach your children and teens that life is precious and that they should respect life.*

Through the portrayal and glorification of violence, movies and television have unleashed a murderous spirit in our nation. Children watch as killers — without any remorse — simply ride away. Young people see this cruelty and begin to wonder if life is precious.

• *Keep in mind that you are an immortal soul, created by God.*

You have no more right to take your life than your neighbor's life. God gives life, and at the time of your termination of service on this earth He will withdraw that life. Man has no right at all to take his own life.

When a person takes his life, he is thrown into the vastness of eternity without God.

> He that overcometh shall inherit all things; and I will be his God, and he shall be my son. But the fearful, and unbelieving, and the abominable, and murderers, and whoremongers, and sorcerers, and idolaters, and all liars, shall have their part in the lake which burneth with fire and brimstone: which is the second death (Rev. 21:7-8).

The time of death is God's business. Man has no right to take another's life nor his own.

• *Remember that Satan is the author of suicide.*

As the "father of lies," Satan will whisper in the ear of a depressed person, "Oh, you'll be better off if you kill yourself."

He is a big advocate of suicide because it is the destruction of God-given life. Jesus said that Satan, the "thief," has only one purpose in mind: to kill, steal, and destroy (John 10:10). The devil hates mankind and desires to take as many people to hell with him as possible.

• *Remind yourself that life is a gift from God, and all His gifts are good.*

I have come across many people who either failed in the attempt to kill themselves or were prevented from doing so. They discovered that life was not so bad after all. Many people who commit suicide would have gotten better had they not taken that final, fatal step.

I have heard about people who go to a pastor for counseling just to make sure they are saved, and then the next day they commit suicide. They want assurance that at the moment of death, they will dwell in heaven. By taking their own life, however, their final act becomes a rebellious sin against God — for which there remains no opportunity for forgiveness.

Let me warn you about this tragedy and emphasize again: Man has no right to abuse the body because it belongs to God. Murder is murder. It is breaking a commandment of God.

Why Do People Commit Suicide?

The reasons people give for wanting to commit suicide are not farfetched, insurmountable problems with no solutions. Most are fairly common troubles that in time will take care of themselves. Here are a few.

• *"I can't live without him."* Although it is fiction, the Shakespeare play *Romeo and Juliet* is a good example of the tragedy of suicide.

When Romeo comes upon the body of his beloved Juliet, he is so grief-stricken, he commits suicide. He would rather be dead than live without her. She later awakens out of a drug-induced sleep, and seeing Romeo dead, *she* commits suicide.

About two-thirds of those who commit suicide for this reason are female. About one-half are in their twenties; 15 percent in their thirties; and 20 percent in their fifties.

• *"I can't live with you"* — A person caught up in a destructive relationship with another person believes there is no way out of the situation. Each seems to bring out the worst in the other, resulting in physical and verbal abuse.

• *Middle-aged depression* — These generally are stable people in their forties and fifties who outwardly are successful but who have inner feelings of meaninglessness and depression. Very often they are concerned about waning sexual prowess and the fear of growing older.

• *Violent men* — Some in this group have had prior psychiatric treatment. They are impulsive, restless, and depressed following a disruptive experience.

• *Discarded women* — These are women who have a strong feeling of having been abandoned by a man. They may have been either rejected or felt they were rejected by their parents. People often don't take them seriously.

• *Malignantly masochistic women* — These women seem to think about death constantly and consider dying an almost welcome end. Some write poetry in which they express death as if it were a lover. Almost invariably, they had an unfortunate childhood.

• *Down and out* — These are men and women whose lives have been a downhill course, having lost a good job or a spouse. Often they are heavy drinkers who become suicidal when they run out of roots in the world. Most have had unsuccessful experiences with various agencies set up to help such people. Eventually, even the agencies close the doors on them.

• *Adolescent family crisis* — Young people in their emotionalism will say to loved ones, "I'll show you. I'll be dead, and you'll be sorry."

Adolescent suicides are often seen as an attempt by the adolescent to dramatize a family problem which invariably exists in these cases. They are often responding to the problems of the family far more than to "drug" effects or college tensions.

Girls have a higher suicide attempt rate, but boys more often succeed.

• *Old and alone* — Often, these people have had stable lives, but in old age they feel everyone important to them is dead and that they have outlived their investment in life. They feel useless, unloved, and are unhappy.

Fight for Your Life

A terrible trend in the past few years is the rise in suicide among young children. A child

138 • The Mystery of Death

should be happy and free, living life to the fullest and discovering God's wonderful creation. Unfortunately, through abuse of one form or another, many children are gloomy, hollow shells who descend into a bottomless depression.

Do not underestimate the devil's hatred. An evil spirit can urge suicide and beg a person to end it all. This is the "job" of a demon.

When Jesus encountered a suicidal man, He realized that demonic powers had driven this man to the point of wanting to end his life. No doubt, this man was so tormented that he felt he was better off dead.

Jesus, however, considered this man's life valuable. He did not want this man to go to hell where he would be tormented worse for all eternity. By rebuking the demons that had bound this man with fear, Jesus delivered him and restored him to his right mind (Mark 5:1-20).

Every time a person tries to think his or her way out of a problem, and hits on suicide as a solution, I can guarantee you it is a demonic spirit doing the urging. A person who is looking for an easy way out of his problems can be deceived into thinking, "Suicide isn't very bad. I can take some pills and go off to sleep."

God does not want you to take your life! Your loved ones don't want you to take your life! In your right mind, you don't wish to take your life — so that leaves only the devil! He alone demands suicide because he knows it is a sure way to separate man from His loving Heavenly Father for all eternity.

The devil will move in on weakness and magnify our sorrows. If you submit your life to God and resist the devil in the name of Jesus, your adversary must flee and the depression will lift.

> Submit yourselves therefore to God. Resist the devil, and he will flee from you (James 4:7).

God does not want our spirits and minds depressed. He wants us to be happy and joyful.

> Why art thou cast down, O my soul? and why art thou disquieted within me? hope in God: for I shall yet praise him, who is the health of my countenance and my God (Ps. 43:5).

Jesus expects us to face up to reality and live life to the fullest. After all, He came to give us "abundant life" (John 10:10).

You are not alone in your journey through life. Along with the presence of the Holy Spirit, you have other sources of guidance and strength: family, friends, pastors, counselors, and God's Word.

God has the power to bring peace of mind to every problem of life and give you joy in living.

> For God hath not given us the spirit of fear; but of power, and of love, and of a sound mind (2 Tim. 1:7).

God gave life, and we have no right to tamper with it; it is His property.

> Then shall the dust return to the earth as it was: and the spirit shall return unto God who gave it (Eccles. 12:7).

We must appreciate our lives until we see Him face to face. When we leave this life, let it be the home-call from God saying, "I've got your mansion ready, come on home."

Until then, we must remain faithful to Him.

Chapter
8

When Your Time Comes

Death is for sure. All humankind has an appointment with death, and there is no escape.

Only those who live to see the return of the Lord Jesus Christ in the air, the members of His Church who experience the catching away as described by the apostle Paul, will avoid physical death.

> But I would not have you to be ignorant, brethren, concerning them which are asleep, that ye sorrow not, even as others which have no hope.

> For if we believe that Jesus died and rose again, even so them also which sleep in Jesus will God bring with him.
>
> For this we say unto you by the word of the Lord, that we which are alive and remain unto the coming of the Lord shall not prevent them which are asleep.
>
> For the Lord himself shall descend from heaven with a shout, with the voice of the archangel, and with the trump of God: and the dead in Christ shall rise first:
>
> Then we which are alive and remain shall be caught up together with them in the clouds, to meet the Lord in the air: and so shall we ever be with the Lord (1 Thess. 4:13-17).

Even these who are exempt from the moment of physical death will be totally changed "in a moment, in the twinkling of an eye."

> Behold, I shew you a mystery; We shall not all sleep, but we shall all be changed,
>
> In a moment, in the twinkling of an eye, at the last trump: for the trumpet shall sound, and the dead

shall be raised incorruptible, and we
shall be changed.

For this corruptible must put
on incorruption, and this mortal
must put on immortality (1 Cor.
15:51-53).

Everyone has an appointment with death,
as Hebrews 9:27 makes clear:

It is appointed unto men once
to die.

We need to be ready for death — our most
important appointment.

When you have an appointment to take an
exam or a test, you will study the material to
make sure you are properly informed. If you have
a job interview, you get ready by being properly
groomed and mentally prepared. If you are to be
married, you prepare for your wedding day by
making sure everything is in order for that appointment with your beloved.

How much more do you need to prepare
yourself for an appointment with death?

Although most of us will have a surprise
appointment with death, we need to be prepared
— mentally and spiritually.

Can any of us somehow change the time of
that appointment? How many people, in the

moments before death, would agree to more time?

Many people ask me, "Is it possible to rebuke the spirit of death and pray the dead back to life?"

Maybe.

The Bible says we can expect to live between 70 and 80 years.

> The days of our years are threescore years and ten; and if by reason of strength they be fourscore years, yet is their strength labour and sorrow; for it is soon cut off, and we fly away (Ps. 90:10).

When the prophet Isaiah told King Hezekiah, who was "sick unto death," to get his "house in order" because he was going to die, the king turned to God and began to weep (2 Kings 20:1-6). God saw Hezekiah's tears and said, "I will add unto thy days fifteen years."

This incident tells us that God did move back Hezekiah's appointed time of death.

The great man of faith, Smith Wigglesworth, asked God for 15 more years when he was 72 years old. He had been in poor health and simply asked God for more time.

God answered that prayer, and at the age of 87, Wigglesworth was still a vibrant preacher.

Then one day, as he was walking in to attend a friend's funeral, Wigglesworth spoke briefly to someone, then his chin suddenly hit his chest. Just like that, God took him.

Fulfilling God's Purposes

When I am called to pray for someone who is dying, I sometimes will ask, "Do you feel that you have lived out the full measure of your days that God put you on this earth?"

If that person says, "Yes, I have finished my time on earth. I am ready to die," I don't ask the Lord to extend his life. I'm not God.

If, however, with a person who is relatively young and who has not fully lived out his days, I come against death. I pray, "Listen, Death, you are a thief, and you are stealing this man's life. According to God, he has the right to live out his measures of days. Step back! I rebuke you by the blood of Jesus Christ — the Saviour who destroys you in the power of the Resurrection because death and hell are subject to Him."

When I was two years old, I had a severe illness that should have killed me. When I was five or six years old, I was saved from being struck down by a moving train. At 17, I was dying of tuberculosis until God healed me. When I was 21 years old, I almost fell into a volcano. That same year, I nearly died of dysentery.

As the late renowned evangelist Howard Carter and I traveled as missionaries across the Himalayas in a mule caravan, we were captured by bandits. The Lord showed us how to pacify our captors with money and food, and they let us go. When we reached the next village, there was a great outcry of excitement at our survival because the bandits had killed everyone else caught crossing their territory that day.

In more than 60 years of my ministry, there have been many times when death came close. None of those encounters, however, "had my name on them." None were my appointment.

I didn't actively seek adding extra years to my life during these situations, but I'm still living. God must have a purpose in keeping me alive.

King David prayed and asked God to let him live long enough to fulfill God's purposes for his life.

> Cast me not off in the time of old age; forsake me not when my strength faileth (Ps. 71:9).

> Now also when I am old and grayheaded, O God, forsake me not; until I have shewed thy strength unto this generation, and thy power to every one that is to come (Ps. 71:18).

We are all living off the divine purposes of God, and I expect to keep on doing it.

My Tibetan Miracle

In addition to my deathbed conversion at the age of 17, I came very near death one other time. The outcome of that experience enabled me to take a glimpse beyond the veil.

Many years ago, while traveling through Tibet with Howard Carter, we were preaching to foreign missionaries, most of whom were from England and Germany.

As in most Third World countries where we had traveled, we knew not to drink the water. We cooked our own food and were very careful in its preparation.

Despite these precautions, I developed Oriental dysentery. It got so severe that I passed blood and ached from head to toe. About every 15 minutes, I was forced to slide off the mule on which I was riding and use "the roadside toilet."

To be a good traveler in many countries, one must not complain. I kept my illness to myself and spent two days hiding my condition from the others. I barely mentioned it in my diary.

On the third day, I lagged behind the others — another big no-no in a country like Tibet. In those days, the mountain passes were thick with bandits. By this time I was almost blind from the fever attacking my body and eventually fell off my mule.

The last thing I remember was tying the mule's reigns to a bush — then I passed out. Three or four hours later, I awoke and realized I was completely well — no need for a toilet, no fever.

I felt so well that I grabbed a stick and jumped on the mule, driving him harder than I had before (maybe four miles an hour!) Catching up with the party that evening, I barely mentioned the reason I had taken so long to arrive.

From there we traveled through China, Korea, Manchuria, Japan, Siberia, Russia, Germany, Scandinavia, England, and several other countries, finally returning to the United States.

While visiting my brother Houston, who was pastoring a church in Mobile, Alabama, a couple from the church invited me to stay at their house. We had a pleasant evening, sitting by the fire and having refreshments.

The lady asked me, "Do you keep a diary?"

A cold chill ran over me as I told her, "Yes, I do."

"Would you please get it?" she asked, specifying that I look up my account from a certain date.

To my shock, it was the entry dealing with my healing in the Tibetan wilderness.

As my hosts and I rejoiced over my miraculous and unexplainable healing, the lady got up and retrieved her own prayer diary.

"On the same day as your entry," she said, "here is what I wrote: 'God told us to pray for Lester Sumrall; he is dying.' So, that is what we did."

At the precise time I was groaning with fever thousands of miles away, this dear couple was praying earnestly that I would live.

When I think about their intercession for me, and God's intervention on my behalf, I can't help but weep over His great love.

Our God is a God of mighty miracles, even to the deathbed.

Flames of Fire

Some people throw their lives away.

A man is a fool to walk out in front of a car. A man is a fool to consume alcohol until it kills him.

It seems a pity to die sick, although we don't always have a say in that. Some people work themselves to death, burning out before they even reach old age. That's an awful way to leave the world.

There is a quality way to die. You can die with dignity and be spiritually healthy, or you can die in humiliation and spiritual deadness.

My brother, Houston, pastored a church in Dyersburg, Tennessee, many years ago. One of the members of his congregation, Mr. Wilson, was the most prosperous farmer in the region. We often visited at his home and ate at his table. A large, hardworking person, Mr. Wilson was quite well off.

He had one child whom he named Bonnie, which means "pretty." She grew up in their Christian home, surrounded by godly people. When Bonnie began to blossom into womanhood, however, a desire for sex rose up in her so strong that she was overwhelmed by it.

One night she ran away from home, taking her clothes and belongings with her. For years her distraught parents heard not a word from her. They didn't know if she was dead or alive. They contacted various agencies, but to no avail.

Late one night, the telephone rang. Mr. Wilson picked it up, and the voice on the other end said, "This is Bonnie."

Mr. Wilson said, "My God, where are you?"

She told him she was in a certain hotel — actually, a brothel — and that he probably wouldn't want to come.

He replied, "I would go anywhere to find you."

Immediately, he and his wife drove to the address in Kansas City.

Mr. Wilson was an enormous man and terrifying if he got angry. When he arrived at this brothel, he was like a lion. He didn't answer anyone when they asked what he wanted. He opened and slammed doors, not caring whom he saw in the process. He glanced in one room and saw a girl who somewhat resembled his daughter. She looked as if she were dying.

He said, "Are you Bonnie?"

She smiled weakly. "Yes, Papa."

He wrapped her in a sheet, put her in the car, and they sped back home to Tennessee.

Upon their arrival, every doctor and medical specialist was called. They sadly told the grieving parents there was nothing that could be done. The family doctor told them syphilis had gone too far, it had eaten her up on the inside.

As she lay in the front room, Bonnie said to her father, "Papa, I am so sorry that I ran away from home. I was ashamed to call because I immediately became a prostitute and contracted this awful disease. I didn't take care of it properly, and now I am dying."

The father tried to encourage her and told her, "God is merciful. You won't die."

"Yes, I will die," she countered. Then she asked him to sit beside her.

The grieving father put his arms around his daughter and begged, "Don't die. Please don't die."

Suddenly, she was startled. "I feel fire coming out of the bed and licking my feet!"

"Lift me off the bed!" she screamed. "The

flames are up to my knees. Higher, Papa — lift me higher!"

Finally, he had her lifted so high, she wasn't even touching the bed.

He screamed, "Ask Jesus to help you!"

She muttered words similar to those the thief on the cross had whispered to Jesus, and then she went off into eternity.

She had been slipping away into a permanent, hideous abode when the grace of Jesus Christ carried her to heaven. As long as there is breath in the body, there is hope.

As long as the mind is alert and there is strength to whisper, the dying can talk to Jesus and have their sins taken away.

Preparing to Die

As he was dying, D.L. Moody, with his eyes open, said he could see earth receding and heaven drawing near.

That, to me, is a quality way to die.

God shows by examples in His Word how to prepare to die and replace the fear of death with expectation.

King David knew he had an appointment with death, but he would not die like his predecessor, King Saul.

Saul stood head and shoulders above his peers — maybe seven or eight feet tall — a giant among men. When God's prophet, Samuel, anointed him as king, Saul was without political ambition (1 Sam. 9:1-10:1).

God changed Saul, and he became a new man. He became not only king of Israel but a prophet as well, and the Spirit of God poured spiritual words and spiritual blessings through this unspiritual son of Israel. When he became a great and powerful man, however, something else changed. Saul lost his humility. He became self-promoting and proud and began to do things his own way.

Eventually, when Saul was at war with the Philistines, he was wounded. Instead of trusting God, Saul begged his own armor bearer to kill him so that he would not fall into the hands of his enemies.

When the servant refused, King Saul fell on his own sword and committed suicide. What a miserable way for a big man to die — lonely and deserted by God on a hillside in Gilboa in northern Israel.

Saul's successor, King David, was well aware of the fallen ruler's shameful death. When the time came, David set his face in Jerusalem to die with dignity. David, thirsting after God to the end, died peacefully, with the honor and respect due a beloved king. There was no shameful end for him (1 Chron. 29:26-28).

154 • The Mystery of Death

The Death of a Rebel

Absalom, son of King David, was a celebrity, a prince, pampered by servants in the palace from the day of his birth. This haughty and proud young man was so vain he cut his hair only once a year.

Absalom never knew what it was to want for any good thing until, in his rebellion, he murdered his brother and was banished from the kingdom (2 Sam. 13).

Even after King David forgave and reinstated him, Absalom said to King David's servants, "I ought to be king in his place. My old man is not dying soon enough. I am going to promote myself to kingship."

Absalom began to meet with the elders at the city gate where business was conducted in an effort to win political clout.

He also ingratiated himself with the people. "Do you have a problem?" he asked them. "I'll help you. The king is too old; you'll never get an audience with him. Tell me your problem, and I will settle it for you."

The Bible says in 2 Samuel 15:6 "so Absalom stole the hearts of the men of Israel."

Finally, Absalom instigated an insurrection and convinced his followers to acknowledge him publicly as king in David's place. But he failed to reckon with one fact — David was God's anointed. Absalom made all his plans, but when he made war against God's servant, he ran into a wire-barbed brick wall.

When the battle went against him, Absalom fled through the woods and got trapped by his gorgeous and luxuriant hair in the bough of a tree. There he hung until David's captain of the hosts stabbed him to death (2 Sam. 18:14).

What a ridiculous way to die. Such a death has no quality.

Today, young people like Absalom, in an effort to reject all authority, speed down highways to fatal accidents that snuff out their lives in one moment of terror. Overdosing on drugs or drinking themselves to death with alcohol robs many young people of the opportunity to die with dignity.

Reaching Jesus with a Whisper

When I was preaching in an auditorium in Honolulu, a physician supporting a sickly-looking man came into the service. After placing the man on a cot, the doctor looked at me and said, "I didn't want to disturb the meeting, but this man is dying and wanted to just hear what you had to say."

"What's wrong with him?" I asked.

"He is a homosexual dying of AIDS."

I walked off the platform and picked this man up in my arms; he couldn't have weighed more than a hundred pounds. His hair was almost completely gone, and his eyes were sunk back in his head.

I carried him back to the platform and began praying for him. I screamed into his ear, "Sir, speak to Jesus! Tell Jesus you're sorry for your sins! Tell Jesus to forgive you of your sins!"

He would mumble because he couldn't speak in a voice I could understand. Finally, he muttered something, and his hand dropped to the floor. The doctor pronounced him dead.

I thought that if the thief on the cross could get his voice high enough to reach Jesus, certainly this man, dying of AIDS, would get the same path to paradise.

Dying Like You Live

In human death, it isn't the quantity that is important, but the quality. I don't mind dying, but I don't want to die the death of a fool. A foolish death can occur out of carelessness and thoughtlessness, as well as out of rebellion and disobedience.

That is why I am mindful of how I live. I do not invite danger. When I visit foreign countries or tramp through the jungles as a missionary, I am careful about where I go and what I do. The same caution applies when I walk on the city streets of America or drive down the freeway.

Why do men die in a certain way? Because

they make certain decisions. We die like we live. In the end, we don't fool anybody except ourselves. If we make wrong decisions, we die in the middle of a wrong decision.

Jezebel was born a princess and lived as a queen when she married Ahab, a king of Israel. Living in a palace where her every whim was law, she had it made. But she was arrogant and mean. No one dared cross her; she was a wildcat (1 Kings 16:31).

Instead of worshiping God and learning how to prepare for her appointment with death, she worshiped Baal and practiced prostitution and murder.

Jezebel's husband, King Ahab, desired to own the next door vineyard, belonging to Naboth, one of his subjects. When Naboth would not sell it to him, Jezebel had the man murdered through a parody of justice.

She treated God's people like dogs, and when Jezebel died she was playing the harlot. Moments later she was pitched from a balcony by her own servants into the courtyard where the dogs ate her flesh and licked up her blood — leaving nothing to bury.

She died as she had lived, in terror and violence, dishonoring God.

That's the Way to Die!

Let's be mindful of a few things:

> • We must die, but we don't have to die alienated from God like King Saul.
> • We don't have to die as defeated backsliders like Absalom.
> • We don't have to die in sin like Jezebel.

We can die gloriously, we can die victoriously, and we can die with divine assurance of a great day ahead. We can die with our faces shining like angels.

There is more than one way to die, as the lives of godly people in the Bible teach us.

Moses sought God's ways and obeyed His voice, leading the children of Israel from bondage in Egypt for 40 years through the desert to the brink of the Promised Land. He helped them, judged them, and interceded for them constantly before God.

The Bible says of Moses, "And Moses was an hundred and twenty years old when he died: his eye was not dim, nor his natural force abated" (Deut. 34:7).

Moses died a healthy, vibrant man.

Like Moses, I expect to die gloriously. I expect to skip right up to heaven. Hallelujah! That's the way to die!

Stephen, the first Christian martyr, was dragged outside the Jerusalem city limits and stoned because of the sermons he preached and the miracles he performed in the name of Jesus Christ.

As the mob hurled rocks, Stephen saw Jesus himself standing in heaven at the right hand of God, and he said, "Lord, lay not this sin to their charge" (Acts 7:60).

The Bible says that Stephen simply "fell asleep" — a glorious way to depart from his enemies in the midst of hatred and violence.

There is a great lesson to be learned here from Stephen's death. When we face persecution, our human nature tempts us to retaliate and try to subdue our enemies. The Lord, however, is faithful to reward a humble and loving spirit such as Stephen's. His decision to forgive his attackers gave Stephen a merciful and peaceful death.

Stephen, one of the church's first deacons and evangelists, met death with a face shining like an angel. In spite of his death's violent circumstances, Stephen was prepared for his appointment. The facts surrounding his death were tragic, but the quality of his death was not. The quality of his death was glorious.

Jesus Makes the Difference

Jesus Christ was acutely aware that He had come to earth to die.

When He was 12 years old, Jesus rebuked

His earthly parents by saying, "Did you not know that I must be about My Father's business?" (Luke 2:49;NKJV).

Later in His ministry, Jesus said, "I must work the works of him that sent me, while it is day: the night cometh, when no man can work" (John 9:4).

Jesus, however, focused not on the *fact* of His death but on the *quality* of His death.

Although Jesus died amid hatred and violence, He knew He would not die like Saul or Absalom or Jezebel. Like Moses and Stephen, He died in close communion with God His Father.

He who had no sin knew the quality of His death would be sufficient to atone for the sins of the whole world. He went deliberately to Jerusalem to die there at His appointed place of execution.

His disciples said, "Don't go!" But Jesus knew what He would do. His "face was set." He knew the quality of His death depended upon His obedience to God's divine will and purpose in His life.

Yes, "It is appointed unto men once to die, but after this the judgment" (Heb. 9:27).

You and I have an appointment with death. We have an appointment with judgment, but Jesus makes the difference. He has set the example for us. He empowers us to live gloriously for God in this world, so that in the judgment, God will say, "Well done."

> O death, where is thy sting? O grave, where is thy victory? The sting of death is sin. . . . But thanks be to God, which giveth us the victory through our Lord Jesus Christ (1 Cor. 15:55-57).

Are you a child of God, on your way to heaven because of Jesus? Are you waiting expectantly for a new life after death?

In death, it is not the quantity that is important, because everyone dies. The death rate is 100 percent. What is important is the quality of one's death.

We must die, but we do not have to die alienated from God, as did King Saul. We *must* die, but we do not have to die rebellious and defeated as did Absalom. We *must* die, but we do not have to die reaping the results of great carnal sins as did Jezebel.

What will determine the quality of your death? Jesus is waiting to change the quality of your death — and your life as well!

Chapter
9

Coping with
Death and Grief

Humans face death in various ways: Some cringe with great fear, terror, and horror. Others shout victory over successfully completing this stage of life and entering a more glorious stage.

Those who cope best with death are those who know Jesus Christ. They accept death as part of life and have their hope placed in things eternal.

Those who cope best with death are those who know what the Bible says about death. Those who know that Jesus became Prince of Life and Death for time and eternity when He rose from the dead will have no trouble facing death when the time comes.

Five Stages

Those who study death have, in recent years, found there are five stages people go through when they find they have a fatal illness. The loved ones of those left behind also go through these same five stages of emotions:

1. Denial.

Even those who accept death as part of life may find it difficult when the time of their appointment becomes real and definite — and not just a theoretical future time. In the sudden deaths of loved ones, this is the stage where people dream their loved ones are alive, then awake suddenly to the reality of loss and feel as if waking up is the nightmare.

Or perhaps they think, *I must remember to tell* whoever it is something that happened. It takes a certain amount of time for the reality of death to be accepted.

2. Anger.

Many people then go through the "why-me" stage, as if death were something unfair — something that only happened to those who "deserved" it.

The next statement usually is, "I don't deserve this. What have I done?"

Death is not a personal affront, a punishment for something done or not done. Death is an inevitable part of life.

3. Trying to avoid or change it.

This is the stage where people facing death try to make a bargain with God. "If you will save me from this, I will do thus-and-so." People seek the opinions of other doctors, seek offbeat treatments, and leave "no stone unturned" to find a way out of that final appointment.

4. Depression.

Once the reality is accepted, many times depression sets in. Grief prolonged can turn to depression, oppression, or suicidal tendencies.

King David in the Bible had a very healthy attitude toward the death of one of his children but not to another. When the child of his illicit union with Bathsheba became ill, he sought the Lord in prayer and fasting until the child died. Then he got up, dressed in clean clothes, and ordered something to eat.

Apparently, in his day, mourning continued for some time, so his servants were totally baffled by his actions. David explained:

> While the child was yet alive,
> I fasted and wept: for I said, Who
> can tell whether God will be gra-
> cious to me, that the child may live?
> But now he is dead, wherefore
> should I fast? can I bring him back
> again? I shall go to him, but he shall
> not return to me (2 Sam. 12:22-23).

Years later, however, David reacted differently to news of the death of his adult son Absalom, who was apparently his favorite. In spite of the fact that Absalom's death had ended civil war in the nation, David mourned inordinately.

The Bible says the victory was turned into mourning because of how David grieved for his son. Joab, captain of David's army, actually rebuked him:

> Thou hast shamed this day the faces of all thy servants. . . .
> In that thou lovest thine enemies, and hatest thy friends. . . . if Absalom had lived, and all we had died this day, then it had pleased thee well (2 Sam. 19:5-6).

David coped with the death of the first child very well, and apparently he had coped with the death of another son — whom Absalom had killed (2 Sam. 13:28-29) — but Absalom's death sent him into a deep state of depression.

5. Acceptance.

What made the difference in the way David mourned for his dead sons? David accepted the other deaths as facts and realities. David's emotions somehow were so involved with Absalom that he could not get above his grief in order to accept the fact that Absalom had died.

When I was a little boy, a man once tried to prove to me that the earth was flat. He lay down on the sidewalk and had me do the same thing.

Then he said, "Now, look, can't you see the world is flat?"

His problem was he did not get up high enough to see the truth. When you fly at forty thousand feet in the air, you can see that the earth is round. The closer you are to the earth, the more you lose your perspective.

The closer you are to the face of death, the easier it is to lose your perspective. To see the reality of eternity, you must go higher in God.

Learning Acceptance

Part of coping with the reality of death is learning how to deal with grief. Grief is our soul's refusal to accept the reality that something is over, things have changed, and we must go on. Grief is feeling sorry for ourselves.

The best way to cope with death — whether it is pending, already has happened to someone you love, or is still an indefinite prospect — is to get to the acceptance stage quickly. The wisest way to do this is to prepare for it in advance.

If a society operated in sensible approaches to reality, you would be prepared for death from the time you were a baby. You would be aware that there already was an appointed time for you to exit this life, just as there was a definite "birth" day when you entered it.

If we were told that death was a doorway to eternity, and the way to prepare for it is to accept Jesus and stay ready to meet Him, there would be no fear of the unknown. You would do your best in this life — and not many people do, even Christians — and when your time came, you would simply go on to heaven.

You would live uprightly before God through day to day prayer, reading of His Word, and developing a relationship with Jesus through the Holy Spirit. Death would be no monster to fear, no "bogeyman" to avoid.

The four stages people go through to get to acceptance of death are tied up with fear. Fear is the enemy of peace. If you love God and know that He loves you, there will be no fear. The Bible says that "perfect love" casts out fear (1 John 4:18). Perfect love gets rid of fear. Perfect love leaves no room for doubt, distrust, or fear.

Fear does not come from God. He gives us a "sound mind," not a spirit of fear.

> For God hath not given us the spirit of fear; but of power, and of love, and of a sound mind (2 Tim. 1:7).

When the Rain Falls

When death affects children — either by

claiming family or friends — it is especially painful. It's hard enough to help adults with the dying process, but if we don't comfort the children, they will continue to suffer for years.

Years ago, children only saw people who were dead when they went to a funeral. Now, children are exposed to death on the evening news, during Saturday morning cartoons, and in theaters. Some experts claim children are becoming desensitized to death and violence. I think the opposite is true — they are more terrified of it than ever.

Children need to be taught that death came upon man because of his transgression against God. We must teach them that God does not want us to die, but that death came about because of man's rebellion. In Christ, however, we are alive.

Children fear the dark, they fear being alone, and they fear death because they have not been taught the truth about being separate from the human body. They need to know that God loves them and He will never leave them or forsake them. God will be with them — even in death.

No matter what age you are now, you can still become prepared to cope with death — whether your own death or that of loved ones.

The sudden death of someone close to you always is a traumatic shock. It is like an earthquake in the mind and emotions. Through a close relationship with God, however, you can soon move to accept what has happened and begin to deal with it.

Fear of death is a carry-over, or a consequence, of sin, and sin is the "sting" in death. Paul wrote that Jesus had removed that sting.

> O death, where is thy sting? O grave, where is thy victory? The sting of death is sin; and the strength of sin is the law. But thanks be to God, which giveth us the victory through our Lord Jesus Christ (1 Cor. 15:55-57).

To be human is to have problems.

To live in a fallen world is to have bad things happen to good people and good things happen to bad people. God said the rain falls on the just and the unjust alike (Matt. 5:45).

Too many people fall down when they have a problem. When adversity hits, they grumble and complain, or mourn and grieve as if nothing but good ought to ever happen to them. That is unrealistic.

Jesus said that He did not ask the Father to take His disciples out of the world but to keep them in it (John 17:15). We must learn how to cope with problems and adversities, how to live through them trusting God to make a way out — not a way around them, but a way through them.

What Is Grief?

When a loved one dies, it is natural to experience grief. But how do you cope with death so that the grief does not cripple you?

When is grief too much grief so that it becomes oppressive and not the release of sorrow?

What is grief, anyway? Grief comes from a French word that means "emotional suffering," or you might say, "emotional hurting." Grief means "sadness of a deep nature" or sorrow.

When you grieve, you hurt. It is not a finger or a toe, but your emotions that are in pain. Your emotions are a large part of the nature of your soul. When your emotions hurt, you hurt all over.

We often say that someone is "stricken with grief," just as we say someone is stricken with chicken pox or appendicitis. In effect, someone's personality has been afflicted with a condition that causes deep suffering.

In the Bible, Hannah's sorrow over her inability to bear a child is described as an abundance of grief (1 Sam. 1:16).

Second Chronicles 6:29 says that everyone knows his own grief. No one understands your grief as you do. Friends or relatives may think they do, but no one can look on the inside of your heart.

I preached the funeral of a small boy in Louisiana some years ago. He was five or six years old and had been run over by a car as he crossed a street. About 300 people came to the funeral, but they never said a word to the grieving father.

As the minister conducting the funeral, I had to stand right beside the father. People would walk by and touch him, but no one said a word. I never forgot what comfort that seemed to bring him. He never looked up, and he never said a word. Just as some grief is too deep for words, some sympathy cannot be vocalized.

This man's friends were so sad for him that there was nothing to say. He knew they were his friends, that they cared for him — but there was nothing his loved ones could do for him.

They could not say, "Brace up!" "Keep your chin up," or any other platitudes to someone who had just lost his precious son. A touch from dear ones, however, helped this father bear his burden of grief. By touching him, they were sharing in his grief.

Causes of Grief

I talked to a lawyer not long ago who said, "You know, Rev. Sumrall, sometimes I don't feel like living."

This was a young man, very handsome, who made a good living, and had a beautiful wife. Their marriage, however, had become a screaming match in which they sought to "downgrade" one another. The love they once had for one another had died somewhere along the way. Now they wanted to "kill" the marriage itself. They not only had anger, but depression and grief.

Grief has been part of history since the Garden of Eden. The Bible talks of grief on almost every page, both in the Old and New Testaments.

One great cause of grief is disappointment, ranging from not receiving the kind of response we expect from someone, to not getting something we wanted. Disappointment is like quicksand. We sink into it, and our personalities change. Sometimes a person's looks change.

The sparkle goes out of the eyes, the lips turn down instead of up in a smile. The person may look five to ten years older. Something happens to the entire person — spirit, soul, and body — as disappointment moves on into grief.

Grief has become a master that seeks to dominate, rule, and crush the person. This can occur through disappointment.

Another cause of grief is losing something we cherish. This kind of grief follows the loss of something precious or the death of a loved one. Anything that is suddenly taken from us that we have considered ours can result in grief.

The death of an unsaved loved one is especially painful. When a loved one dies, and he or she did not know Jesus Christ as Lord and Saviour, coping with grief is harder because there is no hope left.

You, however, still have hope for your life. You must continue to live, and not one of your tears will bring that loved one back. The only thing you can do is to give your grief to Jesus and ask Him to help you accept that this person is lost to you forever.

Until Death Do Us Part

The Bible says when you are married you become "one flesh." When part of your flesh is gone, it can't be replaced.

I buried my father and mother, but it was much harder to bury my wife. I was there when she breathed her last, very peacefully with no struggle of any kind. She went to be with the Lord.

When the undertakers came to take her, I wanted to scream, "Don't you touch my wife! She's my wife. Don't you touch her body."

When they picked her up and put her on the cart, I was almost hysterical, I wanted to scream at them, "Wait a minute, this is her home, this one was built for her, she only wanted to live in this home."

When they started to roll her toward the front door, I really wanted to scream. In my spirit I was saying, "Wait, she belongs here, this house was made for her. This is her house, don't you take her out that door. You must not take her out that door."

God spoke to me and said, "She's not your

wife at all. Your ceremony of marriage to her said 'until death do us part.' "

I said, "You could have extended it, but you didn't." At that moment, I heard death.

"She belongs to me, and she belongs to history, but she does not belong to you," the Lord said. "She is now free of you because your commitment and covenant was until death. And now you're parted. She is no longer yours and has no relationship to you at all, she's mine."

Does time heal all wounds?

I wouldn't know; I'm not healed yet. Sometimes it seems as if I can still smell death in my house. I've changed all the furniture around and done a lot of things differently.

Everything in the house reminds me of something we shared together. Everything I touch, Louise has touched before.

The most difficult time of my life has been since she died. Holidays are hard for me, but my sons and their families all eat at my house.

I go on because if Louise were here, she would scold me. She would say, "What are you doing sitting around? Why don't you get busy and do what God told you to do?"

Hers was a triumphant spirit. I miss her so.

Expressing Grief

Grief sometimes is so intense there is no way to express it vocally. When it gets this deep, it is a "killer." This makes grief harder and stronger.

Some grief can be relieved by weeping. David wept for grief over his enemies. In fact, he wrote that he had cried until his eyes looked like an old man's eyes. They were blurred with crying, "consumed" by grief.

> I am weary with my groaning; all the night make I my bed to swim; I water my couch with my tears.
>
> Mine eye is consumed because of grief; it waxeth old because of all mine enemies.
>
> Depart from me, all ye workers of iniquity, for the Lord hath heard the voice of my weeping.
>
> The Lord hath heard my supplication; the Lord will receive my prayer.
>
> Let all mine enemies be ashamed and sore vexed: let them return and be ashamed suddenly (Ps. 6:6-10).

The Israelites showed grief by tearing their clothes, throwing themselves face down in the dirt, or scooping up handfuls of dust and throwing them over their heads. Other signs were the wringing of hands or rocking back and forth.

Some people in extreme grief have beaten

their heads on walls or pulled out handfuls of hair or beard.

In the United States, a man came for prayer in South Bend, Indiana. He came to our Bible college for some special lessons and we found him sitting on a concrete staircase blaspheming himself about not eating with the other participants. He was beating his head against the concrete wall and cursed himself and kept calling himself terrible names.

Although grief is "natural" and a part of the fallen world, it can become a malignant burden. Grief, left unchecked, can grow like a cancer on the emotions and become just as deadly as a physical cancer.

There are griefs that, if you are not careful, can destroy you. You can bear them so long that there is nothing left inside of you. How can you and I cope with grief so that it does not become this cancer eating away at our souls and lives?

First, analyze the cause of your grief. What caused it? Did a loved one die? Did someone disappoint you?

Once you know where the grief is coming from, seek the Lord Jesus and be willing for Him to bury it. He already took it on the cross.

Jesus Bore Our Griefs

Christians do not have to bear grief. Jesus already has borne it for us.

The best way for Christians to cope with grief is to know beyond the shadow of a doubt that Jesus bore our grief and knows our sorrows, as Isaiah prophesied:

> He is despised and rejected of men; a man of sorrows, and acquainted with grief. . . .
> Surely he hath borne our griefs, and carried our sorrows: yet we did esteem him stricken, smitten of God, and afflicted (Isa. 53:3-4).

How could Jesus bear our grief if He had never known grief? How could He understand a situation he had never been in?

In the Garden of Gethsemane, the evening before the crucifixion, Jesus bore grief. The Bible says He became "acquainted with grief."

I believe Jesus was the happiest person who ever lived because He continuously walked in the will of God. When it came to dying for our salvation, however, He became acquainted with grief.

He could not become acquainted with grief on his own. He never sinned, so there was no loss for him personally to carry. In order to understand grief, however, Jesus had to become acquainted with our grief.

As He knelt in the Garden of Gethsemane,

with the pains and sorrows of the entire world upon Him, Jesus experienced grief like no one has ever known before or since.

This grief was so intense that Jesus' blood came through the pores of His forehead as He prayed. That was physical grief being manifested.

Jesus also knew soul grief. He knew what it meant for one that He trusted to betray Him. As the treasurer for the group, Judas carried the money that was given by others to provide for the needs of Jesus and His disciples. Judas was the most trusted of the Twelve, but he sold Jesus for the price of a slave. That would bring grief to anyone's heart.

When Jesus was arrested and the disciples ran away, Jesus must have grieved. The way Peter denied knowing Him three times while Jesus was being tried as a blasphemer surely cut to the heart of the Master.

Then, Jesus bore grief in His spirit. We will never know the kind of grief He bore on the cross as He took every sin, every sickness, and every sorrow upon himself. That is "redeeming" grief.

Time to Rejoice

Once you have given your grief to Jesus, rejoice in your spirit from that point on. Sing a song, pray a prayer, find a friend to share with. Then you will be able to cope with grief.

If you are grieving over the loss of a loved one who was born again, then it should be easier to give your grief to the Lord. You can be happy that he or she is rejoicing in heaven and has simply gone on to another place ahead of you. It should fill you with joy to know that one day you will see your loved one again.

Be happy for that loved one, even as you are sorrowing for yourself and for your loneliness without them. Rejoice that Jesus is real to your dearly departed. He or she can see, touch, and talk with Him.

Suppose, while on earth, your loved one had been promoted to a high-paying position and given a beautiful home in which to live and never had to want for anything again. If, however, it meant that he or she had to leave and go miles away from you for a time, would you still not be happy for their good fortune?

You can cope with grief over the death of a friend or loved one by dwelling on their present happiness and your future meeting.

When you hang onto grief, no matter how justified it is, you are hanging on to something that Jesus carried at Calvary. You cannot bear the burden of grief by yourself. That is why Jesus did it for you. Be willing to give it up to Jesus.

Lay that grief on Him. Like a baby on a mother's breast, lean on Jesus and say, "Lord, I lay my grief on you."

The peace that comes will be beautiful. It does not matter whether it is the loss of a loved one, the loss of a job, or the loss of a home, Jesus will take it and help you. This may not be easy to do, but it is the only way to cope with grief.

The world has some ways of coping with grief that counselors and psychiatrists will tell you, but none of these can take the grief away. The only method that works is the provision God made for helping mankind with the grief coming from losses of any kind. And that is to let Jesus carry your grief for you.

In a wonderful sermon on the sovereignty of God, Donald Grey Barnhouse used this illustration:

Suppose you are watching a movie. You see a mother and father walking along a road with their child between them. The father hits the child, who cries feebly, "Oh, Daddy, don't!" Then the mother slaps the child, who begs, "Please, please don't, Mommy!" Whereupon the father grabs the little one's shoulders and shakes him. By now the child is sobbing. Oh, what cruel parents, you think.

Then the curtains beside the movie screen slowly open, revealing a wide-angle cinemascope screen. Now you see the full scene: A blizzard is raging. A car, stuck in a snowbank, is in the foreground. The family is struggling up the road toward a house in the distance. The child, half frozen, just wants to lie down and die, but the parents, in love, are keeping his circulation going by slapping and shaking him into wakefulness in order to save his life.

If we could see the full scope of God's screen, we would understand why He lets these things happen. It may be that, as with Job, He is winning a skirmish in the Invisible War. Until we do understand, we just have to believe and trust our Heavenly Father in all that he brings into our lives.

All we can see is a tiny portion of the screen — but we see Him!

You see, my friend, God does see us and care about us. But his mind and plans are infinite, and our minds and plans are finite. We must trust Him to bring about good for us.

Chapter
10

Goodbye, Planet Earth

The Bible says death is an enemy — not a friend. Death robs the young of a productive life. He steals a husband and father, leaving behind a wife and five kids.

A woman with three small children dies. The husband grieves for her, sobbing, "My God, what am I going to do?"

Death is a monster. But he will not have his way forever. God's Word says that death will die. It will be the last enemy destroyed. The Destroyer will be destroyed. There will be no more death.

The last enemy that shall be

destroyed is death (1 Cor. 15:26).

The curse of death will be gone from the presence of God. That is when man will be returned to his created state.

Who is responsible for this awesome power over death? The Lord Jesus Christ!

> Knowing that Christ being raised from the dead dieth no more; death hath no more dominion over him (Rom. 6:9).

The grave has no power over those who have been redeemed by the blood of Jesus Christ. God has destroyed death.

> I will ransom them from the power of the grave; I will redeem them from death: O death, I will be thy plagues; O grave, I will be thy destruction: repentance shall be hid from mine eyes (Hos. 13:14).

Right now, Satan *is* death. He is the one who brings bad things to good people, not God. Because man's sin loosed Satan to roam the earth, we are tied to its boundaries. But only for a time.

There will come a day when Jesus Christ, in power and glory, will come and immediately take charge of this world. Satan's archenemy will lay waste to the Destroyer.

Satan cannot destroy mankind. Why? Because of the sacrifice of Jesus Christ on the cross:

> Whom God hath raised up,
> having loosed the pains of death:
> because it was not possible that he
> should be holden of it (Acts 2:24).

Jesus holds the keys to life and death. Death can't hold Him. God wouldn't permit it.

The Good Life

Those who have had a hard time in life usually die with great bitterness.

I have had a good time here. I have been blessed with a loving family. My mother was a wonderful Christian. My older brother and sisters were eager to be helpful and kind.

Called into the ministry, I felt success from the first meeting I conducted. I went around the world, starting off with $12 in my pocket. Later, I had a hand in building churches, and the money came in without struggle. The same was true with the Christian TV stations we have started.

My life has been good. I had a precious wife for 49 years and eight months — and we never had a fight. We lived in sweetness and harmony without a bitter word spoken between us.

When I say, "Goodbye, earth, it was nice

knowing you," I mean it.

I have no regrets. I have traveled all over the world. I have lived in castles in Switzerland and eaten dinner in palaces. Over the years, I have met many wonderful people.

Everything I have ever done has been a success. I have never failed in anything because the Lord had His hand on my life.

When I say "Goodbye, it's been nice knowing you," it's the truth. I have had a good time here, and I am going on to heaven to have another good time — and probably a better time up there than I had down here! I'll leave this world without any heaviness of heart. I'll leave without any regrets or disappointments.

I'd do everything all the same, and I'd take the same girl with me. It's been a good life and a good time.

Enjoying a Long Life

Thousands of years ago, God set man's time on this earth at 70 years, and that has remained true, more or less, until today. Some people exceed 70. I'm 82 at the time of this writing. My mother was 87 when she died, and my father was 88. My grandfather lived to be about 87. All of my people, for the most part, have enjoyed longevity.

Why have my family members enjoyed long lives? I can't tell you. It could be because they all lived down south where everybody had a garden. We ate fresh food and plenty of it.

My wife's family, however, has a different legacy. Her mother died at 55 and her father at 42. When my wife Louise turned 42 and then 55, she decided it must be time to die.

I shook her and told her the Bible said she was "flesh of my flesh." I told her she had to stay alive, and she did live to be 81.

A lot of people might not believe me, especially at my age, but I don't think about death at all. I may live 120 years; I don't know. I still feel as if I have things to do.

I work harder now than I have ever worked. I preach all the time, and my staff maintains a hectic pace keeping up with me.

One night, we'll be preaching in Russia, then the next night, we'll be in another country. We're away from the States more than we're in them. We move hard, and we work hard.

I'm up by five every morning. I don't have to be, but I enjoy living life. I fiddle around with my writing, preparing sermons and catching up on correspondence. God has blessed me with the energy I need.

No Fear of Death

I hate the word "retirement." Why retire when you've just reached a fruitful place to grow fruit? You've been through experiences that you have to share. You have something to give away. Why die?

Death can cut you short in your moment of harvest. I demand harvest, and I accept challenges today.

I live by faith, and I know that whatever I do, it's going to be good. Why? Because I do it in the name of the Lord. I have no fear of the Lord mistreating me and hurting me. I know whatever He does will be good.

David said in Psalm 23, "Yea, though I walk through the valley of the shadow of death, I will fear no evil: for thou art with me."

We should not fear death.

I don't fear death. In fact, I have a great desire for death because it is the only thing that separates me from the awesome presence of the Almighty.

The stinging dread and dark finality has been removed from death. Through Jesus Christ, the grave is the loser.

> O death, where is thy sting? O grave, where is thy victory? (1 Cor 15:55).

On the cross, Jesus made provision for us to gain back all that Adam and Eve lost. The New Jerusalem described in Revelation is God's next garden — a garden where there will never be a serpent to spoil God's eternal plan for His people.

And I saw a new heaven and a new earth, for the first heaven and the first earth were passed away; and there was no more sea.

And I John saw the holy city, new Jerusalem, coming down from God out of heaven, prepared as a bride adorned for her husband.

And I heard a great voice out of heaven saying, Behold, the tabernacle of God is with men, and he will dwell with them, and they shall be his people, and God himself shall be with them, and be their God.

And God shall wipe away all tears from their eyes; and there shall be no more death, neither sorrow, nor crying, neither shall there be any more pain: for the former things are passed away (Rev. 21:1-4).

I can hardly wait to get to my eternal home.

When My Work Is Over

If you were to ask me right now, "Would you rather die or live today?" I would say, "Die."

But let me qualify that. If Jesus doesn't have my home ready in heaven yet, then it is not my time to die. I don't want to die before my time.

This world is God's workshop. As Christians, we have a certain amount of work to complete here. I'm in my completion stage, working on things God has told me to do. I don't want to be a coward and run to death because it would be easier on me. That would be a selfish act.

Recently, while I was in Europe preaching in three countries, I met with several hundred pastor friends. Because they seldom see an old man in the pulpit, they respect me like a father.

"We need to ask you questions," they said.

"What do you want to know?" I asked, hoping I would have the answers. Even at my age, when a person is supposed to have acquired some measure of wisdom and understanding, there are things I do not completely understand.

Knowing that I can help others, however, tells me I still have work to do here.

If Moses had not heard the voice of God in the desert when he was 80 years old, he may not have lived to be 120. He would have died along the way to the Promised Land. But he heard the voice of God and knew he had a job to do.

Moses finished his work and didn't leave it to anyone else. When the job was done, the Lord took him home.

Life on earth is for those alive now. And I have things left to see through. I don't want to leave behind any unfinished business.

But when my work is completed, I'll be happy to wave and shout, "Goodbye, planet Earth! It's been nice knowing you."